Glass Walls

Glass Walls

Reality & Hope
Beyond the Glass Ceiling

Jean Rostollan and Rhonda Levene

Glass Walls

Manufactured in the United States of America.

For information, please contact:
Brown Books Publishing Group
16200 North Dallas Parkway, Suite 170
Dallas, Texas 75248
www.brownbooks.com
972-381-0009
A New Era in Publishing™

Hardback ISBN: 1-933285-43-5
LCCN 2006923529
1 2 3 4 5 6 7 8 9 10

Dedication

To my parents Mary Ellen and Richard Cross, my
husband Dave, and daughter Cynthia—thank you
for being "Diamonds" and for richly blessing my life.
—Jean

To Tom, for your unconditional love and support,
to my parents, Nealy and Ronald Harris, for setting
the standard for the person I aspire to be, and to Ben
and Matthew, for being my joy and treasure.
—Rhonda

Table of Contents

Table of Contents

Acknowledgments

Throughout our respective and varied careers, we have had the good fortune to work with countless women and men whose integrity and generous spirit have touched us and those around them. We thank them for their wisdom, advocacy, authenticity, and friendship.

Our book has been inspired by many selfless women who, by sharing their amazing sagas, brought life and validation to our project. We admire and respect the courage, passion, and perseverance of these worthy role models, who bring excellence and heart to the organizations for which they work and volunteer each and every day. Without their openness and candor, our book would lack the human connection that brings truth and, most of all, hope for those enduring the Glass Wall journey.

We are indebted to the team at Brown Books, especially Milli Brown and Kathryn Grant, whose guidance and endorsement of this book made it a reality. Milli had the vision to recognize that we had a viable business theory and topical women's issue to bring to light and explore. Through her acceptance of our book proposal, she provided us with a supportive platform for sharing our workplace lessons. Kathryn's availability, support, knowledge, and ready sense of humor turned the entire writing experience into a joy; she exemplifies the positive impact a generous coach has in the work setting.

Finally, to our families and friends, we send our deepest gratitude. Thank you for unconditionally supporting our efforts by offering immeasurable love and encouragement.

Jean and Rhonda

Introduction

Character cannot be developed in ease and quiet. Only through experience of trial and suffering can the soul be strengthened, ambition inspired, and success achieved.

—Helen Keller

◆

Chipping away at the barrier keeping women out of high offices in the business world, females began breaking through the glass ceiling toward the end of the twentieth century.

However, the progress made by women inside the halls of corporate America remains a disappointment for many talented females. While some have beaten the odds and risen to management and executive positions, many say their paths of accomplishment have been a testament to their own endurance rather than a tribute to a progressive and enlightened marketplace. Frustration and disappointment have been the surprise "rewards" for their hard-earned promotions to seats of leadership. In fact, a surprising number of successful, executive women have become so disillusioned that, in some cases, they are choosing to exit traditional corporate organizations altogether and seek alternative career paths. Why, despite their attainment of senior status and the outward appearance of having reached a career zenith, aren't these women feeling professionally fulfilled?

Our study of why this workplace phenomenon exists and how it affects women, particularly those reaching management or senior-level positions, led us to develop the concept we call the "Glass Wall" as one possible explanation. The Glass Wall Theory describes the numbing isolation and unexpected marginalization women encounter when organizations are anchored by a closed group of male elitists.

Until now, the existence of this Glass Wall appears to have been an undocumented truth, a truth that we confirmed through countless interviews with women representing various industries and stages of their careers. The recurring theme of professional disappointment and prejudicial workplace realities proves that the Glass Wall is surprisingly pervasive and transcends all business niches. We hope that a better understanding of the Glass Wall barrier can be a starting point for women trying to navigate workplace challenges and opportunities.

During our efforts to define and refine the Glass Wall Theory, we relied on the fascinating insights offered by many women who shared incidents drawn from their professional lives. Their workplace encounters revealed a wealth of experiences that helped bring some clarity to the confusing office dynamics women are navigating on a daily basis. A particularly valuable insight came from Ellen, a highly placed executive, who shared her life-altering realization. Her personal discovery gives a moving illustration of how the Glass Wall can affect women.

Ellen's Story

Ellen arrived home shortly after 8:00 a.m. on a Wednesday, having caught an early commercial flight from Chicago. Thanks to Murphy's Law and bad weather, she had missed her connecting flight the prior evening and had spent the night at the noisy, overpriced airport hotel. She had no change of clothes or even a toothbrush, as she had only brought a briefcase, a laptop, and her purse. Now, she was in a crunch for time: she needed to prepare for her next cross-country trip and was scheduled to depart in less than two hours. Grateful to be pulling into her cul-de-sac, she also felt a familiar rush of disappointment as, once again, she had missed some time at home with her family. As she opened the front door, she was greeted by silence; everyone had already left for the day.

Glad to have escaped the subzero temperatures in the Windy City, Ellen felt some relief as she savored the welcoming beauty of a sunny day in the South. But she was already tired from her recent string of frustrating hours, and this fully scheduled day was just starting. Entering the sanctum of her bedroom suite, she quickly began preparing for the rest of her day. It was rejuvenating to have hot, cleansing water cascade over her body and then to change into fresh clothes. With a quick shower and her bag barely packed, she heard the horn from the limo that was pulling into her driveway to take her back to the airport.

The remainder of the week would be stressful. Ellen would be entertaining the chairman and his wife of her largest and most important customer, along with the president of her company. Today, she would be flying to separate cities to pick up her guests and then escort them to the U.S. Open in New York. Detecting a sense of disquiet, she couldn't put a finger on why she was feeling so unsettled. It couldn't be the flight schedule. The pilot and private plane wouldn't take off without her, so there was no chance she would miss the flight. It was a luxury not having to race to catch a commercial flight departing from a congested terminal. Since 9-11, traveling via private corporate jet had taken on a new meaning: no security lines, no disrobing for body searches, no unpacking luggage and briefcases for inspections. This plane left when she was ready to go.

During the traffic-clogged commute to the hangar, Ellen contemplated the next few days and how she'd once again be missing the comfort and familiarity of her own home and family. Her regular limo chauffeur was off today, allowing, to her relief, a commute in silence, with the only sounds coming from the voice inside her head. As the black Town Car turned into the gate of the private airfield, she took in the view of the sleek and polished body of the G-7—its steps open to the ground, awaiting her ascent and welcoming her into its private retreat. Ellen, the vision of a confident, well-dressed woman, exited the limo and hurried up the steps of the plane. She nestled into the plush leather swivel chair, adjusted her seat belt, and signaled to the pilot that she was ready. Sitting alone, vacantly peering out the window as the jet taxied into position, she felt something deep within her consciousness suddenly snap. At that moment it struck her—Ellen didn't recognize her own image in her mind's eye. A chilling question surfaced: Who was she? Then a disturbing realization came into focus: her public image and her professional life were in conflict with her core being. Who was this stranger inside her body—and, more importantly, how had this personal transformation taken place?

◆

Ellen is not unlike many of the women who are waking up to a new reality in the fast-paced, political, and "take no prisoners" environment of today's workplace. Ellen's story carries a theme that we heard during numerous dialogues with executive women. Although their specific situations differed, these women shared the realization that a part of them had become unrecognizable, lost, or simply buried. We knew there was a poignant story here, a fundamental problem that needed to be explored.

We started talking about this book five years before we commenced writing. The timeline was delayed because our respective experiences were too fresh, and we were still living the story. During this multiyear interlude, we continued to talk to women, in conversations and formal interviews, about the emerging reality of the American business climate. As these women opened up and shared firsthand experiences, their common themes, emotions, and reactions to events were too consistent to attribute to any single company's or person's idiosyncratic nature. Because these candid vignettes represent actual events, the identities of individuals and companies have been changed to respect privacy. It is not the purpose of this study to target any individual, company or industry, rather to reveal a general problem and search for solutions.

Reflection and soul-searching have been constant for both of us in the last few years. Piecing together our experiences over careers spanning decades has led to understanding and growth. *Glass Walls: Reality and Hope Beyond the Glass Ceiling* is one outcome of our continuing evolution.

We wrote this book to promote awareness of a newly defined business challenge that exists once the glass ceiling has been shattered, to provide some guideposts to assist others on their journey, and to share many true stories of women that we hope will inspire you as they did us.

The Glass Wall

For most of history,
Anonymous was a woman.

—Virginia Woolf, English novelist

◆

In a published survey, 39 percent of executive women ranked corporate culture as the number one reason they left their most recent position. According to The Leader's Edge™, respondents specifically "expressed disappointment in closed management styles that micromanaged and denigrated their work. Many women felt that their roles were not valued and that they were not 'heard' by senior management. Some respondents also expressed that a lack of management integrity that was clearly not in line with their values ultimately led them to change positions."

Statistically, a greater percentage of senior-level women than men will eventually leave corporate America altogether. Rather than continue to sacrifice their talents to an unappreciative business culture, women are choosing to apply their exceptional skills to alternative career opportunities, including self-employment, women-owned businesses, and an array of nontraditional avenues. This shocking level of female brain drain from mainstream businesses is a serious loss to companies whose practices disenfranchise women with valuable aptitude. Shareholders: it's your loss!

The "Glass Ceiling" is a well-recognized problem for working women who are striving to achieve advancement and cope with organizational realities. A Glass Wall is the reality beyond the imposing ceiling—the disillusioning discovery that breaking through the Glass Ceiling neither affords nor guarantees women access to professional equality and acceptance. Instead, after brushing away the shards of the broken Glass Ceiling, executive women metaphorically crash into a new obstacle—a Glass Wall. This is an invisible barrier within the ivory tower, a barrier that surrounds and segregates the inner sanctum of the Patriarchs, the empowered males and their chosen associates who dominate the organization. Females who beat the odds and break into the upper ranks are met with unexpected frustrations as they now find themselves doubly isolated. In their executive roles, they not only experience the "lonely at the top" syndrome; they also are denied the camaraderie of their workplace peers that is enjoyed by their male counterparts. This new barrier is even more challenging, given it is not widely understood or acknowledged.

Glass Wall builders, those men who are not inclined to treat women with the same professional standards as they accord their male coworkers, exist in most organizations. As women enter the upper echelons of businesses and observe firsthand the management styles of the executives, they are validating the suspicion that gender inequalities are still an active force in the workplace. Solid improvement regarding better gender relations appears to be more myth than reality, when you look beneath the surface.

If one female claims Glass Wall isolation, she risks being labeled "paranoid". When numerous women experience access issues, there is corroboration that the problem exists and is not the figment of one person's insecure imagination. Companies that smugly point to diversity programs and the placement of women in their executive ranks have not necessarily addressed the problem. How the women are incorporated into and regarded by the entire management team remain the burning issues. The presence of females in top positions is not sufficient progress, unless these executives have the same access, clout, and opportunity to manage the business as do their male counterparts.

Theoretically, since women are approximately 50 percent of the population, you could conclude that only when a company's total workforce comprises approximately half men and half women has it reached a "labor equilibrium." While we don't advocate a 50-50 ratio across all divisions of a company, we do suggest that equal percentages of males and females in the upper echelons of an organization are reflective of a society's talent pool. Having only one or two females populating the executive ranks still smacks of gender tokenism.

Just as a self-serving fraternal clique or "Patriarchy" managing a company can interfere with healthy business practices, so too can the other extreme, an organization run by and for women, a "Matriarchy." Female-dominated organizations can take on an appearance similar to the Patriarchy. Should the female leadership operate in a prejudicial, elitist style toward men, then, as with the Patriarchal mode, good people are denied equal access to jobs, resulting in a negative environment and potentially reduced corporate results. What this all boils down to is this: inclusion and balance are essential for a productive, salubrious corporate culture.

The existence of a Glass Wall has been confirmed time and again in the situations shared by women from a variety of settings. We spoke to women representing an impressive cross section of disciplines: medicine, research, sales, finance, marketing, manufacturing, legal, high tech, publishing and many others. Regardless of the industry, their experiences are remarkably similar. Why, after the well-earned attainment of senior professional ranks, do these women face disappointment, the lack of validation, little or no support, and ultimately alienation from their male peers? Their experiences validate that the Glass Wall is not imaginary. Furthermore, the sheer volume of their comparable stories points to the existence of the Glass Wall as the rule, not the exception.

The events forming the basis of this book are real and rooted in the professional histories recounted by women who often felt totally alone, even flawed, because of their inexplicable ostracism and marginalization by many men of comparable rank. There is value in this discovery. Recognizing that social and political barriers exist can be the first step in finding solutions. Executive women are not ineffective leaders or a bad investment, despite much propaganda about the failings of high-ranking women. Rather, these remarkable females have faced a Herculean task by dealing with unfavorable circumstances that shortchange the enterprise and compromise business results.

Combining the Glass Wall Theory with a dissection of the Patriarchal methodology leads to a disconcerting insight. Chess pieces on the corporate game board facilitate and perpetuate what in many companies can be described as a Machiavellian form of leadership, a leadership without room for women.

Not all men operate with the self-serving agendas and discriminatory practices of the Patriarchs. Organizational complexity is compounded by various corporate factions and their attendant positive and negative effects on all workers. Women, like their male counterparts, belong to different camps that have distinct attributes and political implications. The mix and profile percentages of the differing entities within the corporate population can significantly affect the likelihood and extent of that company's success.

Hopefully, through exposure to the realities of the Glass Wall, all corporate citizens can find strength, creative solutions, and a renewed inner spirit for the journey to personal fulfillment and professional success. Every day, countless men and women arrive at a crossroads and face three possible options: going in one direction, they can seek human excellence; taking the opposite route, they embark on an unenlightened, backward existence. Refusing to progress in either direction, they will remain at the junction in the road and go nowhere. It's their decision: take the proverbial high road, select the path going in the opposite direction, or remain in neutral and maintain the status quo thereby not contributing at all to the workplace solution. Because all humans are created with free will, how they exercise that will is their choice.

Patriarchs

The queens in history compare favorably
with the kings.

—Elizabeth Cady Stanton & Susan B. Anthony
History of Woman Suffrage

◆

Ask people to recall their junior and senior high school years and list what they did and didn't like about the experience, and the conversation will eventually turn to the variety of social groups that made up the student population. Stratification terms may differ from generation to generation, but what is a universal constant is the existence of basic subgroups within the student body. A breakdown of these social divisions typically included jocks, academics, the middle majority, underachievers, thugs, nonconformists, outcasts, and the proverbial in-crowd, also known as "the clique." This "in" group, which operated as top dogs, could pick and choose some of its select members from the other groups; for example, certain jocks would cross over and have a foot in both camps. Typically, these classmates sitting on top of the social hierarchy became the source for homecoming king and queen, the prom court, and class officers. Usually, the class president was male, whereas the class secretary was female; gender stereotyping was already at play. The exclusive popular crowd predictably had the best record for winning elections and contests, because other students, by their support, thought they had a shot to gain favor, popularity, and possibly stature by supporting the clique's agenda.

As you peel away the layers of how this high-flying inner circle was really perceived by the numerically larger subgroups, what emerges was a genuine disdain for the supposed cool people. Stories surface that cite how many of these elitists were in fact bullies, cheaters, and in general not very nice to those outside their approved social set. In hindsight, the other groups at some point began to recognize that the clique could be highly patronizing when looking for support in situations like running for office but, conversely, distant and even cruel when they had no further need for someone. In the vernacular, clique members were "users."

Now, switch gears to corporate America.

The Patriarchs

Patriarchal ruling societies have existed since time immemorial. A patriarchy is, according to the dictionary, "a form of social organization in which the father is the supreme authority in the family, clan, or tribe, and descent is reckoned in the male line . . . a society, community, or country based on this social organization."

Many interesting analogies can be drawn between the patriarchal form of society and the typical male-dominated workplaces. If you think of the CEO as the "father," and the chosen men within the company as the select clan or tribe, the structures of the two entities are similar. For our purposes, "Patriarchy" refers to the exclusive group of men or "Patriarchs" who dominate the organization, along with the males chosen as their entourage.

Inclusion in the inner sanctum of upper management is a much sought-after prize; power, prestige, and fortune are the rewards for those who reach the top. Only a tiny percent can occupy the upper echelons of the management and officer ranks. In order to get the promotions and support that improve your success and survival rate, a cadre of friendly allies becomes critical. Certain personality types seem predestined for climbing the corporate ladder and commanding a social hierarchy of their making. The top males on the pyramid inevitably establish a buddy system that provides security and stability for them and selected comrades who fit stringent, unwritten membership criteria; they form a "patri-centric" group—a ruling caste. Within this structure, skill sets and management talents do count . . . but only to a point. Shortfalls in a member's intellect and capability can be overlooked if he demonstrates a faithful adherence to the ruling echelon's "platform." What emerges in most organizations is a Patriarchy, which, like the school clique of your younger years and the historical ruling elitists, decides who is in and who is out and grabs for itself the booty of corporate largesse.

Criteria

The Patriarchy fulfills two functions for its members: a business safety net and a social consortium. This group is not open to female membership. Instead, it's a closed group of males whose adherents are chosen based on several qualifications: who is compatible; who is fun; who unquestionably supports the agenda; who reinforces the egos of the fellow members; and who can be trusted. Associates who disregard these primary criteria face banishment. The patriarchy is a friendship alliance that manages the organization. Nonmember employees who hold potentially important positions can be rendered ineffective or removed if not given the Patriarchy's seal of approval.

Entry to this elite club is only for "birds of a feather" who can be trusted. Being trusted is not the same as being trustworthy. Rather, this concept of trust refers to a member's blind willingness to promote and implement whatever business strategy or goal is sanctioned by the Patriarchy's leadership.

Within the group, the Patriarchy is willing to overlook ethical weakness and excuse moral flaws that can be fatal for outsiders. To put it another way, their code of conduct has a double standard. What counts is that a follower is dependably faithful to the official agenda. Any form of opposition—loyal or otherwise—has no place among the members.

Propagation of the Patriarchy is guaranteed, since membership and acceptance by this old-boy system is perceived by many as the best ticket to career advancement. Gain access to the clan, and reap your reward. Once in, a member stays in, unless trust is broken. Members continue to enlarge the clique by bringing in additional reliable pals who, in turn, bring in their buddies. The cycle continues, with its tentacles reaching multiple levels of the organization.

Cronyism

Using a more recognized term, the resulting leadership style is best described as cronyism. The group operates like a fraternity empowered by its control over job patronage. Select members are reinforced and rewarded with salary increases, special privileges, and promotions.

The emotional support provided by the Patriarchy fuels a sense of power, control, security, and fellowship—in short, belonging. The significance of social dependence and security cannot be overstated. A phenomenal bond links the Patriarchs, regardless of what occurs inside and outside the specific organization. Watch the movement of executives within any industry—time after time, the same men will follow each other to new companies. This pattern of migration is, however, not often seen with women.

The more charismatic an individual, the more likely that person will rise through the ranks, as self-promotion is a valuable tool when seeking advancement within the hierarchy. Personal charisma and ability to project power are also helpful attributes when Patriarchs reach outside their own circle to sell their agenda to nonmembers.

Typically, Patriarchs thrive on recognition and, better yet, fame. They rarely miss the chance to attend industry events and will even sacrifice their company's performance to show up at high-profile gatherings. Any opportunity to stand out at industry functions is highly valued, as Patriarchs love being perceived as major players.

Some of America's best known CEOs have shamelessly presided over the implosion of their companies, while living the high life and spending precious time on the keynote-speaker tour. Keeping in the spotlight is a great way to foster cronyism.

Diamond Moments—The Exception

Not all Patriarchal decisions are bad. At times, intelligent insight and good decision-making surface within the executive suite. These are the "Diamond moments," the "aha!" moments, when logical, sound decisions emanate from the leadership. For those who witness such a flash of good judgment, this is a welcome, memorable experience.

Impact

The restricted membership of the Patriarchy ensures that women rarely, if ever, penetrate the inner circle. Although females do break through the Glass Ceiling and achieve high, well-deserved corporate rank, there are often ulterior motives behind the Patriarchy's endorsement. One possible reason for a female's appointment to higher office is that she has performed superbly and possesses the expertise the group is seeking. Certainly, that is an endorsement of her talents. But the downside is that the promotion was probably granted because the Patriarchy couldn't find the requisite skill set among its members. Other women may hold their position thanks to a corporate program established to address diversity demands.

The Patriarchy often approaches the issue of diversity as a numbers game. But healthy institutional diversity is not about window dressing, promoting token, targeted minorities, or establishing number quotas. A valid diversity program opens all ranks to people of differing backgrounds and perspectives; it attracts and hires great talents. New perspectives derived from employees with varying backgrounds and educations enrich the corporate intellectual pool.

Women, because of their gender, are automatically disqualified from participating in the country-club management style enjoyed by their male counterparts. Most female executives make clear that they aren't offended if their male peers socialize apart from them. In fact, the typical woman doesn't see her social fulfillment coming from her workplace associates. What the women do mind is their exclusion from male-bonding get-togethers, during which business issues are discussed and decisions are made. Women are not only denied access to their peers in social settings but are often left out of the management loop inside the office, as well. Impromptu and scheduled meetings that omit female participation are characteristic components of the Glass Wall isolation.

The unofficial business model that results from this fraternal leadership style is one in which corporate vision is nothing more than policy generated from the narrow dictates of an elite group, rather than from proactive, broad-based thinking. With a standard modus operandi in which no one rocks the boat, critical "watch dog" functions and performance audits can be snuffed out. Over time, the company will fall victim to management inbreeding, resulting in a neutered team incapable of designing and executing a solid business strategy.

◆

Sandra, a corporate executive, discovered that although her position was well earned, she wasn't afforded equality by her fellow officers. Despite senior rank, she continued to face Glass Wall barriers in multiple situations inside the office as well as at industrywide meetings. Still amazed at the behavior of her fellow executives, she shares the following experience.

Ditched

The annual conference for Manufacturers' Industry News and Discoveries (MIND) was being held six months after Sandra's company, Central Corporation, had completed its acquisition of another industry competitor. In the past, only one or two Central executives would attend. But now, with a new, expanded list of company officers, five attendees represented the company. It was overkill.

Sandra had been a regular at the event for several years. It was an excellent chance to connect with industry peers, look for ideas that could impact a variety of projects, and hear updates about industry trends. Like most conventions, the event was a blend of social and business activities—a networking opportunity.

Unexpectedly, at 7:00 a.m. on day one of MIND, the phone on Sandra's bedside table rang.

"Hey neighbor, what are you going to do today?" Gary, a company vice president, queried. "Let's compare our calendars."

This is the same Gary who, immediately after the merger, told Sandra he'd like to go with her on any trips she scheduled, so he could "meet your industry contacts."

"Gary," Sandra answered at the time, "I have to believe you have more than enough to keep you busy without adding my meetings to your list. I promise that if it makes sense and the agenda is relevant to you, I'll get you involved."

Now, he was checking out Sandra's calendar again. Clearly, he was at the convention to push his already obvious agenda of becoming an industry headliner. It was annoying.

"Let's meet in the atrium at 8:00. Maybe we can sit together at the presentations this morning." Trapped, Sandra gathered her notes and left her room to meet Gary.

"Any dinners tonight?" he continued to push. "Let's compare notes and see if I have one you might be interested in." Pulling out their appointment calendars and comparing, Gary noted, "Oh, I see we are both going to the Brown Bearings party tonight. They do a nice job. In fact, I've recently become good friends with Duane—know him?"

In fact, Sandra did know him. Although he didn't call on her, she knew he was a Brown Bearings vice president—a comparable position to that of her contact, Allen. To her relief, after the merger, it had been agreed that Allen would continue as the primary sales contact with Central.

Beyond the upcoming dinner with Brown Bearings, Gary's social schedule also showed that he was attending the Acme, Inc. dinner event that Sandra would be attending. "All of us must be invited. Well," shutting his Day-Timer, "it looks like the next two nights are covered." Spotting the other three company vice presidents walking nearby, Gary took off, leaving Sandra alone. Clearly, he had no intention of sitting together at the meetings.

Sandra missed the companionship of Jeffrey, a vice president with whom she had worked for several years. In the past, they often attended MIND together. But Jeffrey stayed home this time around, figuring that it was silly to send one more person in light of the expense; it didn't make sense to have so many leaders away from the business—especially officers whose span of control had nothing to do with the MIND focus. With a sinking feeling, Sandra knew that a new regime, with changing rules of corporate practices, was usurping the culture that Art, the retiring CEO, had so painstakingly created. A newly created Patriarchy was in place, and it was rapidly taking control. As Gary just reinforced, this new peer group talked to Sandra only when they were prying or needed something.

At the end of the morning session, walking between the Renaissance Hall and the Enterprise Building, Sandra was approached by

Duane. Clearly intending to get her attention, he walked up to her, stopping her for a chat. "I'm not sure how to say this, but ... Sandra, we don't have enough seats for everyone tonight at the restaurant. So I need to uninvite you from the Brown Bearings party. Sorry. There just isn't room." Shrugging his shoulders, as if to show it was out of his hands, he turned and briskly walked away. *This is a first!* If she was the one in charge of the event and seats were limited, she'd insist that a junior salesperson not attend and give up his seat for a good customer!

The afternoon sessions passed quickly, possibly because during the fifteen-minute breaks, her mind was preoccupied with the insulting request not to attend the Brown Bearings party. The topics covered that afternoon were relevant and invigorating. The seminars were in plain English and instructive. Under normal circumstances, it would have been an A-plus afternoon.

Racing back to her tenth-floor room at the conclusion of the final session, Sandra had little time to spare. She changed from her business clothes into an evening party dress, checked her makeup, gave her hair a quick touch-up, and left for the hour-long cocktail party. This party, open to all attendees, was usually the best opportunity for reconnecting with industry peers in a casual setting.

The composition of tonight's crowd reinforced the usual male-female percentages. There were maybe two or three dozen other women in attendance, whereas there were four or five hundred men. As usual, the cocktail party was easygoing—ideal for unofficial deal-making. The liquor flowed, and the fancy appetizers were ample and delicious. At least, though her dinner plans had been bashed, she wouldn't starve tonight.

Toward the end of the MIND cocktail hour, while sitting at a bar in the lobby with some acquaintances, Sandra had a front-row seat to observe the four Central Corporation officers—Leo, Gary, Ben, and Stanley, along with a phalanx of Brown's sales-men—line up for the limo transfer to the party. The scene was a visual definition of cronyism. One thing was clear: the whole "uninvite" was a setup.

Thanking her friends for the conversation and a final round of drinks, Sandra decided the best way to end the evening was to catch up on phone messages; make a few calls, including her nightly travel call to home; and, at some point, order a late snack from room service. If after eating she was still lucid, she'd curl up with a good book.

After touching base with her family, Sandra ended her evening in typical fashion. She was alone, while the guys were living it up with their buddies. Calling her friend Nancy, Sandra recounted the strange events of the day.

"Just when I think I've heard it all, you go and surprise me," Nancy winced. "It's déjà vu. But what gives this an interesting twist is the being 'uninvited' part. That defines the concept of rude; it's a new one on me! I'll bet you anything that, as we speak, those guys are drinking cognac and tripping over themselves to impress each other. The Patriarchy is so predictable!"

"How are you feeling about it right now?" she continued.

Sandra couldn't forget the embarrassing and belittling scenario. "I'm hurt and incredibly angry." Continuing with her emotions rising to a pitch, "I feel like I'm surrounded by some sort of force field. If someone attempts to reach out to me, they get zapped. It's preventing me from any meaningful contact with these men. It doesn't make sense from a business perspective—it's a chronic, ridiculous reality."

"Look, I decided a long time ago that I don't need to have my peers as part of my private social life. I'm OK with that. But I *do* deserve respectful treatment," Nancy added.

"Same here. Just don't push me away when it's business." Sandra agreed.

Day two of the convention followed the same pattern of sessions, lunch, and more sessions. Again, the official activities were capped off with the usual cocktail party, designed to encourage mingling and conversation. This was the evening Gary confirmed that he and the other three male executives were going to the Acme dinner. Optimistically, Sandra thought she could catch a ride with them. This time, no prearranged limos or buses were lined up. To get there, the attendees would need to grab a cab for the crosstown trip. Turning around to place her empty glass on a tray, Sandra looked at the revolving hotel doors just in time to see her four fellow officers hail two cabs and take off for the dinner. *Ditched! And on purpose!*

"So what did you do?" Nancy asked during a phone conversation later that night.

"Simple—I hailed a cab and went to the party by myself. It's clear. At these meetings and more and more in the office, I'm on my own."

Sandra still recalls how frustrated she felt that night as she talked with her friend—it was a tough period in Sandra's career. Not only was she dealing with Patriarchal-induced frustrations in the office, but she faced some blatant cronyism at industry functions as well.

"Because I traveled and attended industry functions, I had a chance to talk with other women. My saving grace was discovering they were dealing with circumstances that were a carbon copy of mine. It really helped knowing that I wasn't alone—that other female professionals were facing strikingly similar frustrations," Sandra recalls. "These fellow sufferers became a valuable resource, a real alliance of women with experience-based suggestions on how to deal with our similarly challenging situations.

"Don't get me wrong, this is not to say that all males conduct themselves in an arrogant, self-important manner," Sandra adds. "Over the years, I've met some talented, highly functional men who were wonderful to work with. To this day, some remain part of my valuable network.

"But, on the flip side of the coin, there were constant reminders that many of my peers operated as members of an exclusive male club. Oftentimes, their show of respect and consideration toward me was more for managing their public image than any genuine attempt at professional inclusion. These guys were masters at projecting whatever persona was necessary to make them look good, even though their real actions often reflected a totally opposite reality."

◆

Strategy—Striving for Excellence

No one ever said that dealing with difficult personalities is an easy task. Coexisting and flourishing in a company manned by the Patriarchy is especially challenging, since these are the people in power.

Women who are newer to the work setting can find a lot of wisdom from those with more "time and grade." Experience can provide a road map and a valuable tool chest, so that you have more options and insights into dealing with the Patriarchy. The input of seasoned women suggests the following blueprint.

First, a measurable, strong work performance is your best starting point for pursuing both advancement and a meaningful coexistence with the Patriarchy. Don't check your female qualities at the door! Instead, recognize that research validates the fact that women bring valuable components to the corporate table. The only competency on which women score lower than male counterparts is self-esteem. Therefore, a top-notch job performance buttressed by an ongoing accumulation of knowledge is your first strategy for creating effective career growth and a sense of personal self-confidence. If you find a void in your grasp of any relevant discipline necessary for successful performance, seek out anyone at any level in the organization who can teach you what you need to learn. Most people love to share their areas of expertise—after all, it's good for everyone's ego to be sought out and to feel valued.

Second, you need to be a source for solutions—a catalyst. Enthusiasm is contagious. If there's a problem to solve, use a fact-based approach with your boss or peer. Suggest: "Here's a possible solution or alternative. Let's talk through it." This strategy is what the best salespeople use. They don't sell a product; they sell a solution! Present new clear options, thus giving your counterpart or boss the opportunity to change his or her mindset or approach. Never be afraid to present your case. Over time, it gets easier. By doing so, you stand to gain respect and recognition for being an informed resource, an asset to the company.

Third, if there are issues affecting your position or status, it's best to address the matter directly. An example could be lobbying for a position for which you've been overlooked as a candidate. Approach the subject openly with the decision maker. Ask that person to help you understand why the position is not available to you. Sell your candidacy by focusing on solutions that you bring to the table, rather than by insisting that this job is something you're owed. By presenting your credentials and performance results, help *facilitate the decision* in your direction. Nothing is worse than never trying to influence outcomes. Obviously, you can't expect a hundred percent of the results to lean your way. But if you continue to make your case, your odds will improve. It's like playing golf. The ball will never reach the hole if you don't send it forth with enough momentum to reach the target. Find the same energy to move yourself forward at work. It's a mistake to remain passive and think you'll get noticed and therefore don't need to devise an action plan. Become a healthy competitor and seek out opportunities to present your value to the decision makers. But don't make the mistake of turning your campaign into a personal agenda. Avoid being a rebel without a cause. Neither you nor anyone else benefits from that tactic.

◆

There are other forces at play in every company, but they don't get the attention they deserve. The lonely isolation imposed by a Glass Wall can be lessened when you discover that the office contains an amazing group called "Diamonds." When women in the workplace recognize the Diamonds—those males and females who embody human enlightenment and represent the best qualities that can be found in fellow workers—they discover a valuable on-site resource. Understanding Diamond characteristics can facilitate finding and accessing these high-caliber associates who can become the "wind beneath your wings."

Diamonds
Mining for Mentors

We don't accomplish anything
in this world alone . . .

—Sandra Day O'Connor

◆

Great leaders are blessed with a magical combination of intrinsic qualities that result in priceless acumen. You have only to look at the past to see timeless examples of such people. Abraham Lincoln, Mohandas Gandhi, and Eleanor Roosevelt were exceptional people who managed extraordinary times by relying on instinct. The roots of these famous pathfinders were diverse, and their early years were marked by both achievements ranging from modest to disappointing; but their ultimate impact on events was earth-shattering. Individuals of such stature are rare and valuable—both in political settings as well as in business.

Every day, on a smaller scale and in varying degrees, unrecognized leaders are plugging away inside countless companies at all levels of the organization, operating on an entirely different mental plane than many of their fellow high-profile executives. Whereas the Patriarchy can readily choose to enlarge its pseudo-family circle, genuine talent standouts don't propagate in the same fashion. Typically, they are much more limited in number than the members of the higher profile old-boys club, because, in many cases, these leaders are born, not made. If you envision the concept of leadership as a continuum of talent and effectiveness, at one pole are the Patriarchs; anchoring the other end are diligent employees with a strong work ethic, steeled by a moral backbone that sets them apart from the multitudes. They are like diamonds—precious, rare, timeless.

A diamond is the hardest matter found in nature; its physical properties make it one of the most sought after substances in the world. In addition to its highly valued industrial applications, when this compressed-carbon element forms as a gemstone, it is greatly prized for its beauty as well. A diamond can cut glass.

Various attributes determine how a diamond is valued and used. Some stones go to consumer markets, others to manufacturing applications. As gemstones, diamonds have varying degrees of clarity, color, carat weight, and cut. Certain diamonds may appear to be perfect on the surface, but a closer microscopic examination reveals flaws that reduce the intrinsic value of the stone. Many of these flaws are "OK" from the retail-market perspective. They make the diamond affordable for jewelry, because to the unaided eye, they are still sparkling and beautiful. They don't have to be perfect. Look at any jewelry display case. Of all the gems, it's the diamonds that stand apart from the others due to their brilliance.

Likewise, look at any business organization—it's the Diamonds who offer the most leadership potential and significant talent. From the Patriarchal perspective, corporate Diamonds have a serious flaw: they aren't candidates for Patriarchy membership because Diamonds march to a different drummer; hence their opposite location on the leadership continuum from the Patriarchs. Diamonds are excellent employees without hidden agendas. If Diamonds don't feel that their ethics and independence are compromised, they can coexist with the Patriarchy.

Diamond Characteristics

Standards

Diamonds are open to paradigm shifts, as they are not locked into a singular view. They are zealous when it comes to demanding a high performance standard from themselves and others. They save their respect for individuals who pull their own weight and make legitimate contributions to the entity for which they work or volunteer. Diamonds are not afraid of objective performance measurements. They are suspicious of anyone who is.

Mentors

Diamonds have a natural gift for sharing, coaching, and questioning. In the role of mentor, they are exceptional. This is a talent that cannot be replicated by way of the executive- or human resource-imposed advocate, buddy, or mentoring programs. Diamonds are open to new ways of doing tasks and typically welcome any opportunity to push themselves and others to a higher level of knowledge and performance. They empower people. They welcome the victories and achievements of fellow workers, as Diamonds inherently know there is unlimited success available for everybody.

Feedback

A logical extension of being a natural mentor is having solid communication skills. Diamonds recognize that all perspectives have potential nuggets of wisdom and welcome input from any source. As a result of their accumulating data, Diamonds are good at analyzing and solving problems. On the flip side of the coin, a Diamond's verbal feedback, even if sparse, is done effectively in a meaningful, clear, and respectful manner. Diamonds have a talent for defining goals and effectively seizing teaching moments. Communication-challenged individuals are unlikely to solidly fall into the Diamond camp, as they are saddled with the inability to fully gather and objectively synthesize complexities. As a consequence, they cannot present clear solutions and strategies.

Independent

This characteristic alone will keep a genuine Diamond out of the Patriarchy. Diamonds aren't motivated by the need to belong to a group. This doesn't mean they are antisocial, but it does reveal a personality that finds motivation and fulfillment in ways other than acceptance by some sort of "in group." Fueled by an inner drive to do what is right versus what is popular, Diamonds are apolitical employees.

Trustworthy

Diamonds are ideal "safe harbors." Their open-door approach, guarantees that, if requested, information will remain confidential, assuming that the request is appropriate and that no one is in danger of harm. Because they are independent, competent coaches and communicators, Diamonds can serve as resources for brainstorming and troubleshooting in professional and, in some cases, personal areas.

Objective

Diamonds exhibit analytical thinking combined with instinctual "gut feelings" when making decisions. Their motive is determining what is most beneficial for the company, rather than for the power clique. The Patriarchy, if operating with any business savvy at all, should value input from a Diamond. Conversely, the ivory-tower clique can also feel threatened, because apolitical Diamonds make perfect corporate watchdogs and, in extreme cases, whistle-blowers. Diamonds have built-in radar for ineptitude and fraud.

Inclusive

Males and females have equal opportunity for Diamond status. Therefore, it should not be surprising that these stellar performers are blind to gender and have respect for ethnic differences. Diamonds see quotas as a phony effort to make public-relations points. Instead, they practice *real* diversity. They welcome input from a broad spectrum of people, knowing that the best approach to problem solving is eclectic, taking the best ideas from diverse sources. Diamonds don't hire clones, because they don't have the need to surround themselves with yes-people or pools of like-minded individuals to give them strength through numbers.

Devoted

Diamonds are devoted to a company's product and purpose more than to a specific group of people within the organization. Consequently, although a Diamond may be dedicated to Company XYZ, this commitment is neither blind nor boundless. If events lead to a conflict with his or her conscience, a Diamond will take the higher moral ground and, for preservation of inner peace, use these differences as a catalyst to move on to other career opportunities. However, when allowed an uncompromised playing field, Diamonds are company enthusiasts—and give 100 percent.

Affable

The affability of a Diamond isn't necessarily the most important character feature. However, this corporate contributor can work with virtually any individual or group of people, because the Diamond focuses on high standards, mentoring, and quality feedback. Although Diamonds are characteristically civil while being forthright, don't expect strong social amiability from them.

While some Diamonds may have a warm and welcoming style, that trait exists only if it's a genuine attribute. Diamonds don't strive for social or political acceptance. That would be putting up a false front.

One caveat: the affability of the Diamond can be strained and even disappear, if the individual is forced into a bogus setup to sanitize an event or a performer's record. On these occasions, the Diamond's watchdog instincts take over. They want no part of a "show trial."

Unselfish

Unlike the Patriarch's ego-driven focus on self-promotion and legacy, a Diamond readily recognizes others' contributions and successes and does not measure personal achievement by the trappings of inner-sanctum glamour.

Balance

Diamonds don't rely on the management cliques at the office for their identity. Freed from the political affairs that are eating up others' emotions and objectivity, Diamonds have more emotional freedom and personal energy for family and other arenas, including volunteerism.

◆

The vast majority of successful corporate women attribute portions of their advancement to those special individuals—Diamonds—who in a variety of ways "made a difference" in their work life. It might have been the boss who had a special knack for teaching the ropes, or the peer who gladly shared knowledge and resources. Many women cite a strong role model who insisted on the incorporation of challenging standards and, in the process, pushed them to attain higher levels of expertise and productivity. Several women also noted special Diamonds who had the courage and insight to take a chance and give these aspiring females a once-in-a-lifetime opportunity for promotion and responsibility.

Why aren't these amazing Diamonds running more organizations? For one thing, Diamonds don't possess the narcissism needed to fuel a personal campaign for attention and advancement. They don't focus on promoting themselves through attending conventions or seeking high-profile situations that offer a stage for individuals striving to become corporate bigwigs. In addition, many Diamonds are women, a group that regardless of talent or style is automatically denied total access to male peers and many plum positions inside the ivory tower. Diamonds, by rising above many politically charged situations, aren't inclined to play the games and kowtow to expediency; they aren't willing to deal with the entanglements that would result from the subjugation of their souls. Whereas Diamonds are valuable resources to a Patriarchy hoping for a solid company performance, they don't fit the Patriarchy's criteria for insider faithfulness and, therefore, aren't in line to enjoy the spoils of the Patriarchy's patronage system.

◆

Anna and Becca share a story of how they first met more than twenty years ago and the challenging circumstances they've encountered in their respective careers. Anna credits Becca for being both a mentor and a role model, who, despite conflicting pressure from a boss, chose to hire and promote Anna into her department, based not only on Anna's professional attributes but also on Becca's gut instinct that looked beyond the surface.

"Becca is a perfect example of a Diamond," Anna states. "She took a calculated risk by adding me to her team. I knew I had met a woman of tremendous substance as soon as I joined her staff. Also, it was through her sharing of some of her disillusioning experiences that I began to realize that women, even if immensely talented, can be overlooked by the male power structure and surrounded by a Glass Wall.

"There's good news in all this. To this day, Becca and I have remained friends, despite going our separate ways in business. Becca is living proof of the value of networking. I still seek her advice on any number of things!"

Becca

Anna had worked in Quality Assurance at Grove Products for just shy of two years. Although she thoroughly loved the department and found her boss, Sam, to be a terrific leader, she knew it was time to pursue a chance to apply for a posted internal job opening; this position, if she secured it, would give her a chance to tackle more responsibility and advance professionally. For the past several months, Anna had felt a diminishing sense of achievement; her work no longer provided the intellectual stimulation and challenge her mind sought. Ready to apply for what appeared to be an interesting promotion into the Finance Department, Anna suddenly bumped against an unexpected quandary: she discovered she was pregnant.

Thrilled to be expecting but at the same time discouraged by the timing of the pending event, Anna wrestled with her options. Stay put? Keep her pregnancy a secret and still apply for the position? Talk to her boss, discuss the job opening, and level about her personal status? Each scenario had a downside. The first would derail her need for professional advancement by prolonging her stay in a job she'd outgrown; the second would technically be legal but somehow felt deceptive, since she'd be hiding a pending six-week leave; the third would be open and honest but pose a potential liability for her candidacy if other applicants had equal skills and no family-planning issues.

She chose the third course of action, deciding to openly discuss with Sam her decision to apply for an internal posting—and sharing her news about the pregnancy. Sam reacted predictably, with the admirable characteristics that made him a Diamond. With his blessing and support, Anna applied for the analyst position.

Rebecca, a director at Grove Products, was the highest placed female in the organization. Smart and industrious, she was, by all descriptions, a real dynamo.

Known for her sense of humor and approachable style, "Becca" effectively conducted the interview, which clarified the job description, noted how the responsibilities related to the department and the company, and assessed Anna's responses to all the questions. One thing was clear: Becca had high expectations. Impressed by the candidate from Sam's department and somewhat surprised by Anna's candor regarding her pregnancy, Becca carefully considered the different applicants and came to the conclusion that her first choice was Anna. Despite being counseled by her boss, Matt, that hiring an expecting female was nothing short of idiotic, Becca was convinced after several follow-up meetings with Anna that this was a woman who was serious about her career and would return to all responsibilities after the arrival of the baby. Becca, risking Matt's disapproval, took the chance and hired Anna as her new financial analyst. Anna, impressed with Becca's open-mindedness, felt that here was a truly insightful person, since Becca was much more interested in Anna's analytical skills than in her maternity status.

Moving into a new department with energizing responsibilities was all Anna hoped it would be. However, it soon became clear that an additional learning opportunity was emerging. Anna was observing firsthand the challenges, both trivial and significant, faced by a female executive like Becca. While Anna was absorbed in learning all the new analyst functions, including numerous audit projects and countless spreadsheet analyses, she was also tuned in to the intriguing dynamics plaguing her boss. An incident at one of Becca's management meetings was illustrative.

Becca's organizational position required her to attend and update the company executive forum, made up of officers and directors. Typically, this summit was held on the first Wednesday of each new fiscal quarter; however, rescheduled to a Thursday, the upcoming session was being held at a private country club close to the office. For the attendees, a special event was added to the agenda: after the meeting, they would spend the afternoon playing golf.

Arriving at the club on the designated Thursday morning at 8:00, Becca proceeded to the fashionable conference room, which was connected to an equally nice restaurant. The plan was to complete the meeting, have a light lunch, and then be on the golf course by 1:00. Showing up with her golf bag tucked away in the car trunk, Becca was looking forward to a break from the pressure-cooker projects and the chance to rub shoulders with the guys.

With her usual reliability, Becca's update was smoothly delivered and contained well-conceived recommendations. Moving on, successive department heads detailed their quarterly update. With polite civility, the group applauded each portion of the program. Knowing that tee times were at stake, discussion was shallow, brief, and succinct—the entire room focused on staying within the four hour window of time. The final presentation moved along and, like clockwork, ended at 12:00 on the nose. The executives hungrily moved into the dining room, chatting and joking, eager to eat. Lunch was casual: a basket of chips, a sandwich, and the usual assortment of soft drinks. There'd be more refreshments on the course during play, when the roving beverage cart would refresh the thirsty golfers with an unlimited beer supply. At 12:30, the president thanked the attendees for an insightful meeting and wrapped up the quarterly exchange. Not wasting a single moment, the company directors went to their cars to retrieve their golf bags and prepare for tee times.

Wrestling her clubs out of her trunk, Becca heard a nearby voice.

"Becca, didn't they tell you? Thursdays are always Men's Day here. You aren't allowed on the course."

"What? I just participated in a company meeting, so logically if the company meeting is continuing with a round of golf, I should play just like anyone else."

"Sorry—it's not going to happen. They don't make exceptions."

"Did the organizer know this was the rule when the date was determined?" came her exasperated reply.

"Oh yeah, Ralph knew. It's his country club."

Another director, who was parked next to Becca, chimed in. "Hey look, Becca, I bet if some of us band together, maybe we can get the country club to make an exception." With that suggestion, the majority of the directors became mute—ostriches with their heads in the sand. It wasn't their battle, so they weren't going to fight it. Two of the more astute, open-minded men quickly formed an alliance and, approaching the club's management, insisted on Becca's right to golf with her male counterparts.

Becca was grudgingly allowed to golf that day—but as she and Anna discussed years later, the whole exchange was symbolic of life in the executive lane. Even though many country clubs eventually dropped their "Men's Day" and laws have been added to the books prohibiting certain discriminatory practices, concealed prejudice against women remains a factor in corporate America. Diamonds are rarely the ones running the companies.

◆

Diane's experience with juggling complex corporate personalities and conflicting agendas illuminates how managing both problems and opportunities assertively may be the best methodology for managing your career path. Along the way, she experienced the pleasure of working with gifted mentors—Diamonds. These positive encounters contrasted with the stress of dealing with company favorites, whose connection with the Patriarchy gave them license for questionable conduct. Her story, which follows, shows that Patriarchs can have rare Diamond moments.

A Diamond Moment

David was the president of Global Industries and the boss of Clarence, Diane's newly appointed abrasive, sexist boss. Diane knew the men had a history, although she was unsure of the specific connection. David was at least twenty years younger than Clarence. Diane didn't give it much thought when David called, requesting a meeting; she assumed he was looking for a marketplace update. Recently, Global had encountered an aggressive competitor, and Diane's team had developed a creative strategy to insulate their customers from the predicted onslaught of sales pitches. By all measures, not only were their tactics working, but as a side benefit, they were generating incremental profits for her team.

Entering the elegant hallway of the top floor was like being in the stratosphere. Diane always felt like she was breathing thin air. As she approached David's office, he motioned her in even though he was finishing a call. Sitting at a round table at the opposite end of the office from his desk, so as not to inadvertently eavesdrop on his conversation, she had a full view of the L-shaped room. Positioned in the northwest corner of the tower, the executive suite had a breathtaking panorama of the company campus and miles of lush woodlands. The well-appointed sitting area outside David's office was larger than her living room at home. While she gazed out the windows, she heard David say, "That's what I need you to do . . . Call me back when you get it done." Hanging up, he rose from his high-backed green leather chair and walked to the conference table.

"Thanks for coming on such short notice. I wanted to talk with you about the recent management transition. So how are things going with Clarence?"

"It's been interesting. He has a very different style from his predecessor, Kathryn."

"OK, Diane—so tell me, what do you really think? How long did it take before you and Clarence butted heads?"

Diane had always appreciated David's laid-back approach, which led one to believe he sincerely wanted to know one's thoughts.

"Oh, I'd say it took about the first minute of the first day he came in. I'm sure it had nothing to do with his calling me by someone else's name—not once, but twice during our first staff meeting—and then telling me in front of a peer that he didn't care what I thought."

David leaned back in his chair and heartily laughed. "That sounds like typical Clarence. You have to understand something about Clarence. He's ex-military. I doubt he's changed anything about his management style from the day I first met him. You know, Clarence hired me into the company."

Now things are starting to make sense!

"No, I didn't know that."

"Look, I need you to give him a break. He has a lot of good qualities, and I can always count on him to make the numbers."

"David, how may I ask did this come to your attention?"

"It's not really important. But I did tell Clarence that I'd kick his ass if you resigned while working for him!"

It didn't take a rocket scientist to figure out that either Kevin, who was Diane's competitive co-worker, or Clarence himself had filled David in on the events over the last few days, during which Clarence had repeatedly belittled Diane during strategy meetings. Diane knew that while she was in David's presence, she needed to keep her emotions in check. She couldn't tell if David really cared about her or was more worried about a harassment claim. In spite of his "regular guy routine" she wasn't quite certain he was genuine.

"David, I love my job and this company. I really care about how people are treated. But I'm entitled to have a voice about what happens—you're not paying me big bucks to ignore problems."

"Listen Diane, I was on the phone with Pete when you came in. Pete runs the manufacturing plants for me. I know that when I pick up the phone and tell Pete to do something, he will. No questions asked. It's the same way with Clarence. Let me assure you that you have a voice and that your opinion is important. I've watched your team and believe that you are one of the best people managers in our business. But I need you to find a way to work with Clarence."

The rest of the conversation was devoted to discussing strategies for battling the competitor. David confided to Diane pending changes in the organization that would improve the company's ability to respond to the changing marketplace. They made sense and sounded on target. Leaving David's office, Diane hoped that even if Clarence was a problem, there was a possible ally in David.

After Diane's conversation with David, the following months proved that some of the changes he confided to her did indeed happen. For her part, following his advice, Diane continued to manage her conversations a little better with Clarence. He still had influence in the organization and, to quote Kevin, "was better connected than God." Her efforts met with limited success. There was obvious tension, particularly in company meetings, where Clarence never failed to embarrass her or disregard her opinions. Clarence's abrasive treatment was becoming a fine art. His knack for testing the limits and stopping just before breaking the ground rules that would place him in trouble with David was getting old. Diane steeled herself—she was not going to let this beat her!

Diane had checked in with Kathryn, her mentor and prior boss, on the topic of Clarence and was surprised to learn that Kathryn was in a similar hostile situation, despite her elevated executive role and status in the company. There were senior leaders in the company who were determined to bring her down. Her influence was growing and they felt threatened. Rather than devoting 100 percent of her energy to productive corporate initiatives, Kathryn was trapped into ridiculous game-playing.

"Some days I wonder when these skirmishes will escalate and become an all-out war," Kathryn sighed, clearly frustrated to hear that Diane was battling the same demons.

Diane always looked forward to attending the large industry convention in Las Vegas. It was a great time to entertain customers and exhibit the company's newest products and services. Jim, one of her managers and a travel companion to this meeting, especially lived for these events. Anyone could tell he was in his element with customers; he loved what he did and it showed. During the plane ride, Jim confided in Diane that he wanted to be an officer of the company by the time he turned forty. Now, as he was approaching thirty-eight, he felt that everything was on track. In her role as managing director, Diane was responsible for identifying and developing talent—mentoring and promoting top employees like Jim. From what she could see, there was no reason to believe that Jim wouldn't reach his goal.

As Jim and Diane made their way to the convention hall, he asked, "So, are you going to go after the new vice president position in our division?"

Diane knew about the position from her earlier conversation with David. "I'm definitely interested," she replied.

"It seems to me that you have all the right credentials and would be the prime candidate. I know Kevin thinks the position is going to him."

Diane stopped abruptly. "How do you know that about Kevin?"

"He told me so himself. He's told everyone on his team, too. He said that David has promised the job to him—it's been fully discussed. Diane, I thought you should know before it's too late. You're twice the leader he is, and everyone knows it."

Kevin, her fellow director, had proven himself to be slippery and downright dishonest on several occasions. Since Diane didn't condone his actions, she usually laid low, and tried to avoid interaction with him. He was Clarence's boy—untouchable. Still guided by her parents' teachings, Diane believed that people like Kevin would eventually be found out and would suffer the consequences. She was disgusted by how the managers around him emulated him, almost to the point of idol worship. It was sad and disturbing to watch.

Diane really wanted the new vice president position. It was a perfect fit and would be the culmination of all she had been working for. This promotion would mean she had broken into the exclusive club as an officer of a public company, a world-renowned one at that. Adding to the lure of VP status, this position would allow her to influence the people and culture of the organization; it offered a huge chance to "make a difference."

Thinking over a possible strategy, Diane noted in general how differently the two sexes approach situations and weigh in on office politics: men don't seem to have a problem with being direct; women, on the other hand, tend to adhere to the rules, respect the chain of command, and try to make things work for everyone. Females are much better consensus builders. Diane clearly followed the female mode of management. But she began to sense that a more assertive approach was now necessary. Operating in "survival mode" as of late, she found that her ability to be direct was increasing proportionately with her growing experience.

As Jim and Diane walked through the convention hall, greeting customers along the way, she continued to mull over her options. Later that night, there was to be a small reception that David would be attending, along with some other industry executives. Perhaps this would be a perfect informal opportunity to approach David—if she decided it was the right thing to do. She needed time to assess her options.

Returning to her hotel room to check in with the office and catch up on paperwork, she figured she had two hours to work and would still have some time left for her daily exercise routine. After wrapping up what odds and ends she could, she quickly changed into her running clothes. With ninety minutes remaining, she could squeeze in a few miles before she had to shower and change for the evening. She entered her "zone" as the plush glass elevator took her to the first floor. Seeing no one she knew in the lobby, she headed out the front of the hotel to the strip.

The sidewalks were teeming with pedestrians at that time of day, making a measured paced impossible. At the first corner, she turned and headed down a side street that offered her a clearer path and a sunset view. Running was a solace to Diane. She had taken it up after college, mainly to help her watch her weight. It turned out to be something she felt born to do. Physically and emotionally, it was a salve to any day she encountered. When she was running, her clarity of thought often led to some of her best ideas. It was her most effective thinking time.

If I go directly to David tonight, the situation with Clarence could get even worse. Kevin would go ballistic. He already thinks he's won. Somehow, I need to make my intentions clear—I need to enter my candidacy into the competition. There's no way this game is over yet. No way! Diane's consistent jogging pace was increasing into a brisk run.

There had been many tough moments in her career, but she had managed to live through all of them. Now, with the open officer position at stake, those past situations seemed inconsequential. *Maybe I should call Michael and get his take on the situation.* She had kept up with his career as he moved around Europe and Asia with Global. His consistent workplace mentoring and support had made him one of the most influential people, along with Kathryn, in Diane's career. He could be counted on to be a solid sounding board, and also he knew all the players.

Broaching the topic tonight is probably a bad idea. I need to remember that patience is usually a virtue. She turned a corner, running rapidly, and soon was in sight of the intersection that would take her back to the hotel. *I need to wait. I should probably talk with Clarence first, not to ask permission but to give him the courtesy of letting him know my interest—just to keep him in the loop, so he has no reason to be upset when I then talk with David. I may even score some points.* The final turn came; her run was three-fourths over. Returning to a more measured pace, she continued to define a game plan. *I will definitely call Michael first; he may have some thoughts that could make a difference. Then I'll talk to Clarence and from there make an appointment with David.* The hotel was now only a few blocks away. *After all that, I'll ask Kevin to lunch, as a courtesy. He needs to hear it from me that none of this is about him.* Back inside the hotel, she walked along the side walls of the lobby, hoping to avoid anyone she knew, since she was in workout clothes. Grabbing the first elevator, she escaped to the sanctum of her twenty-third-floor room. Her daily run ended and a plan was formed. It needed to be executed over the next three days.

Her brief conversation with Michael took place very early in the morning due to the time zone difference in London. He had been in England for several months, and by all reports was flourishing. He was always encouraging and supportive. In agreement with Jim's strategy, he told her to go ask for what she wanted.

"There's no downside to asking, Diane! It would be a pity not to ask for what you want and then lose a prime opportunity because the right person doesn't know you're interested," Michael counseled. "But stay tuned in to Clarence. He has a lot of deep ties at Global and isn't above making your life miserable." Diane had no problem believing Michael's feedback. This man was reliably honest and had finely honed instincts.

The meeting with Clarence appeared to go as expected. He listened to Diane explain why this opportunity would be the right one for her and what she could bring to the position. She could sense his mind churning away. If she were to get this position, she would have more power but still be in his organization. Clarence would have to continue to put up with her opinions and watch his step. He had not enjoyed being somewhat muzzled for the last months. He could refuse to support her, but that would be political suicide in a company trying to encourage and promote more women. He even had a bonus objective tied to diversity.

"You know, Diane, there's a vice president position open in our sister company right now. I could talk to the president and put in a good word for you." Diane's radar picked up on this one right away. He wanted her to leave, and this was a way to look like he had helped her. Diane also knew about the VP position with the sister company. That company was an "old boys" network like none other. *From the frying pan to the fire!*

"Thanks, Clarence. I appreciate it, but I'd like to go for this position. I was thinking about setting up an appointment with David to discuss his thoughts about me as a candidate for the role."

"You can do that if you want, but I'm pretty sure someone has already been identified for this job."

"Well, I'd like to try anyway."

Diane left thinking that just when you believe the man can't get any more devious, he does. Was she that bad to have around?

Outstanding business results, happy and talented staff—just what was the problem?

The meeting with David was even more enlightening. He seemed appreciative that Diane had taken the initiative to set up the meeting.

"Diane, I know why you're here today. You want to talk about the new vice president position in your division."

"As a matter of fact, I do. Is that all right with you?"

"Absolutely! Let me share with you my thinking in creating this position."

David proceeded to outline his plans for the division. With double-digit growth over the last several years, its size was becoming cumbersome to manage through only one key leadership, which is to say VP, position. He wanted to reorganize the division in a way that would support and bring focus to the most profitable segment of Global. Clearly, David needed to keep this one winning branch of the company healthy—his management design was logical. This made perfect sense to Diane. She knew that other areas of the company were having tough times. Unlike Diane's division, the company's overall growth rates had been declining the last few years, and profit margins were being attacked as aggressive competitors gained market share.

"David, you know I've held positions in four different departments in Global. Right now, I'm really enjoying running a business unit. It gives me the complexity and intellectual challenge I love.

Managing the M&A department was a great way to learn about our business, but having frontline responsibility and being held accountable is an excellent match for my abilities."

"I can't deny it—you've done an outstanding job. Your team continues to meet every goal thrown at it. Initially, I wasn't comfortable with your transition out of M&A to a business unit, but both Michael and Kathryn couldn't say enough good things about your capability. You proved me wrong."

"Thanks, David. It's always nice to hear positive feedback. Michael and Kathryn gave me many opportunities to develop; without their backing and trust, I wouldn't be sitting here today. I've tried to follow their lead by creating a culture that people can thrive in. I know that you may think this job's a stretch for me, but I'm convinced it isn't." Then, pausing a moment, she continued, "I've also heard that you might have someone else in mind who, to your way of thinking, better fits the profile for the role."

"That's interesting. I do have someone in mind, but I haven't made my decision yet. I'm not sure if he is ready. Frankly, I'm also not sure that this VP position is the best next step for you. Let's look at another possibility. Diane, I'm having a problem with one of our key distributors. I don't have anyone who really understands the financial and business side enough to work through the issues. What if you agreed to handle this negotiation, in addition to your current responsibilities, and then at some point in the future we talk about your next steps?"

"Isn't the distributor located in Boston?"

"Yes, it is. I'd guess we'd be talking about a minimum of twelve months to navigate through the issues and reach an agreement. Sometimes, it's been done in nine months, but other times it's been closer to eighteen."

"And let's say I accept this interim job—what happens at the end of the completion of this assignment? Would the VP position be mine?"

"I can't make you any promises. We'd just have to see then."

"OK, let me see if I have this right. You basically want me to live out of a suitcase for the next year, taking on an assignment with multimillion-dollar implications for the company, *in addition* to my current responsibilities, and proving to you a skill that you already know I have—with no promise of a VP position when I'm done." *Does he really think I'm that stupid?!!*

"That's right. It's an important assignment, and I don't have anyone else I can tap. I could maybe see about having someone taking over your team in your absence."

"David, if I can't negotiate a better deal for myself than this, then I don't deserve the VP position."

"Well, you got me there." He leaned back in his chair and rubbed his temples. "This puts me in a difficult position, because I already promised the job to someone else."

"David, we both know you're talking about Kevin. He's shared your promise to him with others."

"Dammit! That's exactly why I don't think he's ready—a lack of leadership."

"I have found sometimes a lack of leadership is a cover for other issues as well."

"I know the guy really well, Diane! We started at the company together. I know he's got an integrity problem."

"David, if you know that, then why are you considering him for a key leadership position?"

"Because he's great at what he does, and the customers love him."

"Hmm, it's obviously your decision, David. I know that I can do this job, and I want this position. But I also know that I don't want to spend the next year living out of a suitcase. I can't believe I'm the only one that could handle this issue with the distributor."

"You're probably right. OK. Look, let me think about it, and I'll get back to you sometime next week. If nothing else, I do appreciate your handling the Clarence issue delicately for me. You may not believe this, but I think he's becoming your biggest fan." *You're right about that. I'll never believe that Clarence is now or ever will be a "fan."*

The last piece of Diane's plan was a one-on-one conversation with Kevin, letting him know that her interest in the vice president position was nothing personal against him. Like any career-minded individual, she was applying for a position that was her logical next move. Around her, he had kept his supposedly pending promotion close to his vest; now it was time to get this thing out in the open between them. Unsure of how he'd respond to her lunch suggestion, she was pleasantly surprised when he readily accepted. On neutral ground at a local diner, at first it looked as though they could hold a conversation that was fairly open. Perhaps this lunch wouldn't be a total disaster but a starting point, maybe even a success. But things went downhill, as it became clear that the sense of competition she felt from Kevin was very real. He believed that the only way for him to succeed was for her to fail.

"So you think David is going to create two VP positions?" Kevin sneered.

"I'm just saying that anything is possible. You and I don't necessarily want the same things."

"Oh, you're telling me that you're not interested in getting a big corner office with your name on it?"

"Kevin, that depends on what I have to sacrifice to get it. I like having a personal life, too. Some of the senior VPs travel constantly and rarely, if ever, make their kids' soccer games. I don't want to be that way. At some point, there are other considerations for me. I still believe that people are most effective when their lives have some balance."

"You can say anything you want. I don't believe you. I know you met with David and made a plea for my job."

"Kevin, did it ever occur to you that it might be 'my' job?"

Diane could tell she wasn't breaking through. The erected wall between her and Kevin was too great to climb over—their entire approach in the workplace was just too different. To Kevin, she was the enemy. She had been unrealistic to think she could have an open, productive discussion with someone locked into such a win-lose mindset. They ended the lunch with an uneasy truce, agreeing to act civilly toward each other in meetings and to keep their disparate views and commentary between the two of them.

David surprised the corporate echelon with his surprisingly enlightened, unexpected decision—Diane's promotion to vice president.

"Looking back, I remember having mixed emotions—feeling excited and scared at the same time. But the political undercurrents in the division were still there. Getting the job was only half the battle. Keeping it and thriving in that environment was the other half. I knew that not everyone would want me to succeed." Diane continued, "Having an officer's title was great. But for me, this achievement was more about recognition and respect for my work and dedication to the company.

"Additionally," she added, "I was so thankful and fortunate to have Kathryn, Michael, and Jim as sounding boards. Not everyone has such supportive resources inside their place of work. They're treasures.

"I hope my story encourages other women to take a proactive role by asking for what they want and endeavoring to level the playing field at work. Even the Patriarchy can't always afford to ignore well-presented facts—and on occasion may have a 'Diamond' moment."

Strategy—Mining for Mentors

Occasional Diamond moments by Patriarchs should not lull one into a false sense of security. True Diamonds are the unsung heroes in corporate America. Their mental agility and contributions to an enterprise cannot be overstated. Hence, Diamonds are a significant resource for anyone sincerely desiring a network of talented individuals and a standard to emulate. The benefit of being Diamond-aware and welcoming them into your circle is multifold.

First, as mentors, Diamonds are an excellent resource for accessing knowledge: a critical building block for a strong job performance. They can be excellent tutors for anyone looking to enlarge his or her data bank. Look both inside and outside your reporting structure to find these stars. Connecting with them, regardless of their department affiliation, furthers your opportunity to have a more global, informed perspective, which in turn deepens your problem-solving capabilities. There are many ways to access Diamonds, but you should initially look for one-on-one settings. Suggest a lunch or make an appointment, so as to have quality time to get their input on a project or proposal. Recommend their inclusion on special project teams. Always reciprocate by offering them any expertise you may have. Just as they are contributors to your knowledge bank, be available to offer them the same assistance. A good relationship is the most fruitful when it's a two-way street.

Second, the qualities that Diamonds bring to an organization make them ideal role models to emulate. Your leadership can benefit from adapting their operating style.

Third, a connection with Diamonds should help women feel less isolated. Since Diamonds don't have a political agenda, they also don't have any objection to freely interfacing with men or women in executive offices. The "Lonely at the Top" syndrome can be mitigated, at least in a business sense, by the intellectual assistance of a Diamond. You can count on them for their availability and honesty.

Ultimately, introducing Diamonds to your world can only occur if you become adept at recognizing a Diamond when you see one! They don't wear any special sign or uniform to make them readily obvious. Instead, you should keep in mind their classic set of characteristics, and you will eventually hone your ability to detect the Diamonds in your midst. Keep in mind the summary of "Diamond Criteria" (see chart on page 58) as you seek men and women to add to your consortium of reliable associates and coaches.

◆

Not all workers can be described by the characteristics of the Patriarchs or the Diamonds. To assess further how best to function in a corporate environment, knowledge of other groups is valuable. So far, two behavior extremes have been dissected. Now, the remaining groups populating the office need definition and discussion.

DIAMOND CRITERIA

Characteristic	Diamond Quality
Standards	Establishes high, measurable standards for self. Strong work ethic.
Mentor	Revels in success of others and recognizes that their achievement is good for entire organization. Natural mentor and coach.
Feedback	Consistently absorbs and provides feedback in a respectful and timely fashion.
Independent	Is not motivated by need to belong to a power clique. Secure with self, giving the Diamond the ability to do what is "right." Unwilling to take positions because of political expediency.
Trustworthy	Keeps confidences. Not interested in the gossip trail.
Objective	Makes decisions based on solid business grounds.
Inclusive	Is "blind" to gender and ethnicity. Assesses a person's worth based on one's contribution to corporate goals.
Devoted	Enthusiastically champions the company, but is willing to detach and ultimately depart from the organization that expects participation in questionable or unethical assignments or behavior.
Affable	Works well independently and in groups.
Unselfish	Instinctively gives credit for projects to those who did the work. Knows there is plenty of success for everyone.
Balanced	Respects the need for both a successful business experience and a home life.

Seeds, Informers, and Corks

I want to let you women in on a secret I've learned through my years in the corporate world: There is a set of unwritten rules in business and, while you may not choose to follow all of them, if you don't know what they are, you might as well be playing the game with both hands tied behind your back.

—Gail Evans
Play Like a Man, Win Like a Woman

◆

Multiple work-team personalities create the texture of a company's playing field. The organizational hierarchy and its idiosyncrasies are less mysterious if you understand the operating styles of various business subgroups. It's especially valuable to recognize how different personality types, Diamonds included, interface with the Patriarchy. This insight is empowering and can make it easier to navigate the corporate maze, avoid unnecessary pitfalls, and form more positive relationships. In other words, to maximize your personal and professional effectiveness, know the lay of the land at your office.

Assessing an individual's group affiliation facilitates comprehension of their modus operandi and puts often-predictable behaviors into perspective. Glass Wall–isolated female executives might partially mitigate their exclusion by more targeted and customized workplace networking that promotes an awareness of and a strategy for dealing with these different worker psyches.

Other Corporate Groups

All sorts of personality and talent types populate the worker ranks. If a relatively small percent of a company's employees are members of either the Patriarchy or the Diamonds, then logically the majority falls into other stratifications. While some of the staff more closely identifies with the extreme poles populated by the Patriarchs on one end and the Diamonds on the other, most workers fall into a category called "Seeds." These Seeds are plentiful, have a variety of talents, and can flourish, barely survive, or die, depending on their environments.

Other individuals operate in a style that reflects more of a host-parasite relationship with the Patriarchy. These two distinct personality types are "Corks" and "Informers." Each of these classifications has a predictable dynamic with the Patriarchy.

Although men can fall into any of the classifications, women cannot. Therefore, in this chapter, "Women" also form a group.

What becomes interesting is how the five groups are viewed by the Patriarchy. For the ivory tower, Seeds, Informers, Corks, Diamonds, and Women each fulfills a corporate purpose.

Seeds

Seeds are those workers who, on a day-in-and-day-out basis, bear the burden of running a company. They are the taproot of the organization. By performing an entire spectrum of tasks, these individuals are the "sweat equity" behind a company's success. Although they rarely, if ever, have input into long-term planning and strategizing, their efforts implement the decisions handed down from Mount Olympus.

Seeds are a valuable collection of individuals, as they blend together to form a moderate majority. Without this middle-of-the-road workforce, there would be an insufficient talent pool and virtually no "farm team" to populate the countless jobs that become vacant or are created as an enterprise evolves. This same group is also a valuable buffer between opposing factions. They bring sanity and balance to the extremes.

Seeds are the initial source for the Patriarchy, Diamonds, Informers, and Corks. However, most Seeds will remain planted in the neutral zone. Either they don't have access to or they aren't driven to identify with any particular clique. Some Seeds work simply for a paycheck, while others love or hate their job. Regardless of the emotional attachment to the company, typically Seeds perform their job, collect their wage, and go home. Unless they are seriously provoked, they stay under the radar.

> **Strategy:** Mentor these individuals and become their role model. Just as they provide a significant resource for the company, they can also become a valuable network for anyone willing to take the time to cultivate their strengths. Look for these "Diamonds in the rough," as they are a potential source of dedicated, honest workers, if nurtured.

Informers

Informers are panderers, Patriarchal wannabes. These individuals, male and female, are "covert operatives" and provide propaganda and insider information to their managers or executives. In a sense, they are spies and saboteurs who hope for personal gain or favor by providing their eyes and ears to the leadership. They operate like a sniper with no regard for his or her victims. They aren't concerned that their feedback can hurt others. Informers use their carefully groomed connections to deflect attention from their own ineffectiveness or shortcomings by casting blame for their problems and performance issues on innocent coworkers.

Informers can also become overt in their actions. They may flaunt their connections with the leadership and revel in the supposed power this affiliation brings. The Patriarchy can use these overt operatives to implement unsavory, unpopular actions, knowing that the Informer is more interested in appearing anointed by the ruling clique than worried about any negative reaction from the rank and file. If holding a management position, an Informer may be called upon to relocate or even fire a worker that the Patriarchy has targeted. Feeling immune from any fallout, Informers typically operate as if they are "bulletproof."

Informers reap rewards from time to time, as they may get salary increases or even promotions. After all, the Patriarchy needs to reinforce its sources. But because Informers have a tendency to be loose cannons and thrive on the gossip circuit, they will never win the big prize of inner-sanctum acceptance. Inherently, Informers can't be trusted, which makes them a potential liability for the Patriarchy. But since they can be "in the know" as to what is happening in the ranks and are allowed access to the upper echelon, informers are misled to believe they have a toehold in the ivory tower. They are users who, in turn, are used.

If the Seeds or Diamonds become aware of an Informer's role, the Informer will likely be avoided or, even worse, ostracized. Savvy, competent workers don't respect these opportunists. Like in school, no one likes the brownnoser. Consequently, Informers may ultimately end up with no allies within the organization—a self-inflicted loneliness. If there is a change in command, Informers can kiss their supposed prestige and power good-bye.

Strategy: Never underestimate the ends to which Informers will go as self-serving operators. These manipulators are masters at projecting themselves as your ally, when, in fact, they are anything but. When teaming with these individuals, remind yourself that it is not necessary to like everyone with whom you work. Recognize that Informers probably have some intellectual expertise that is valuable; so don't hesitate to draw from their knowledge bank. By understanding from the beginning that Informers have unethical motivations and methods, adapt your communication and business methodology accordingly.

If you become aware of an Informer's activity, be proactive! Counter the Informer's propaganda efforts by providing well-documented, objective information to the Informer's contact person. If nothing else, by sharing your enlightened feedback with various executives, you develop improved relationships with them as well. Facts are your ally! Encourage objective performance measurements for you and your staff.

You are well-advised to pick your battles when dealing with Informers, letting little things go and focusing on important issues. Avoid contending with these agents, as they can be convincing martyrs and will only step up their espionage efforts if they feel threatened. Nurture their sense of value; they love feeling important. In the long run, karma will deal with these toxic people.

Corks

Corks are males who automatically agree with anything the Patriarchy chooses to do. They are enablers. From the Patriarchal perspective, this personality type makes for an ideal member on the Board of Directors, since a Cork's unwavering support for management is a given. Corks are the "B-team" for the Patriarchy. That is to say, within their ranks are the future members of the inner sanctum's uppermost executive layer. A Cork doesn't have the fortitude to disagree with upper management; as to a spineless Cork being a whistle-blower—forget it. Not a chance.

Strategy: Having a positive relationship with a Cork can be helpful; their endorsement is a valuable plus if you apply for other corporate projects or positions. Conversely, their ire can block your career advancement. Be cautious with Corks, and remember that these are not individuals in whom you should confide. They have a strong tie to the Patriarchy.

Since Corks are not independent thinkers and can be self-serving workers, they are not ideal coaches. Corks can provide corporate insight, as they are more likely than most to know what's going on with the upper ranks; but gather their input through active listening rather than with an exchange of your opinions.

Diamonds

While Diamonds hold great potential value for the Patriarchy, a Diamond, by virtue of integrity, independence, gender (if female), and other character qualities, can never be a member of the in-crowd.

Strategy: Diamonds are fabulous coaches and teammates. They are worthy members for any project team. Invite their participation and input whenever possible. Remain apolitical with Diamonds (as well as with the other groups). Through emulating a Diamond's behaviors and expertise, you can become a more knowledgeable, impactful, and valuable leader.

Women

Women can fall into one of three groups: they exist as Seeds, Informers, and Diamonds. However, they are excluded from two others: Corks and the Patriarchy. Some women may erroneously believe that they have garnered unqualified social and professional parity. However, unless they are in the unlikely situation of working for an organization run by Diamonds, genuine acceptance by and equality with the Patriarchy is an illusion. Over time, these misled female executives will start to discover that they have been covertly excluded from various meetings, social events, and conferences. Eventually, like all women dealing with the Glass Wall, they will realize that they are denied a position on the real playing field.

◆

Most of us know the feeling of taking a vacation from work *physically* but remaining mentally saddled with issues at the office. The bad news is that you can, in fact, be unable to fully relax during the few precious weeks per year while on hiatus. The good news is that different settings can provide a more objective, nonthreatening environment for serious soul-searching. Clarity and inner peace can come when you least expect it.

Silver Lake Epiphany

Following a long-standing family tradition, Theresa and her family went north to their lake cabin to celebrate the July 4th holiday. For both Theresa and her husband, it was an annual escape from the trials and pressures of their jobs and a chance to enjoy uninterrupted time with children, siblings, and grandparents.

With fireworks and parades over, the next morning Theresa awoke just before daylight, unable to shake her habit of getting up by 5:30 a.m. With her husband and children sound asleep, and the rest of the family exhausted from all the holiday activities, she made her way to the quiet kitchen, brewed a cup of coffee, and set off toward the pier, where gentle waves lapped against the wooden structure positioned on the south side of the bay. Dangling her feet in the cool, clean water, Theresa leaned against a support post, positioned to observe both the dramatic sunrise unveiling in the eastern sky and the early-morning activity on the placid lake. As beautiful as the sunsets were over Silver Lake, the early dawns were equally breathtaking; both phenomena were ideal for deep thought and introspection.

This midsummer break had come not a moment too soon. Capitol Industries' dysfunctional team and its unimpressive results had created an air of desperation in the executive offices. No one had a clue what to do or how to go about generating turnaround results, which the company so desperately needed. The malaise was pervasive. Communication was at an all-time low, as the overwhelmed CEO remained myopic, still operating as though he was running a private fiefdom—not a scenario likely to placate the Seeds or encourage their continued hard work in the corporate fields. Theresa sighed as she pondered all the craziness. How had such a promising organization gone so wrong and become so inaccessible to her?

As she sipped her lukewarm coffee, pondering the origins of the decline she feared would destroy a once-remarkable company, Theresa noticed a small bobbing object floating ten or so yards off the pier. After a fish jumped nearby, the spreading concentric waves created by the movement of its reentry caused the beige item to move and sway with whatever direction the water's motion took it. As it gradually floated nearer, pushed by a combination of the current and the light breeze, its identity became clear—a small, cylindrical cork—probably from an exploding bottle of champagne someone had aimed toward the lake during the prior night's celebrations; it was now floating lackadaisically.

Theresa's eyes continued to follow the cork. Regardless of the motion of the water, the wind, or jumping fish, the cork never sank. It stayed afloat, nodding in whatever direction nature pushed it. It wasn't anchored; it had no definite path. The cork merely bobbed and swayed, totally subject to its environs. Were it to meet a huge wave or be submerged by an encounter with a boat, that little bottle stopper would eventually return to the surface, simply because it was a cork. It didn't have to think about how to overcome a drenching, the jumping fish, or the recreational traffic. It was impervious to the water and indestructible, always righting itself and continuing its directionless existence, its presence contributing nothing to the ecosystem of the lake.

Grimacing, Theresa realized that the qualities and characteristics of her fellow executives seemed to figuratively have the same DNA as this cork. Like the innocuous beige floating plug, the executives with whom she worked merely nodded and bounced about with the currents. Neither those humans nor this inanimate object did anything constructive. They were rudderless, literally going with the flow, never taking a fixed or strategic position. No matter what was thrown their way, they merely bobbed back to the surface, as if in agreement with the new circumstances, to survive again and again, their buoyancy being the unavoidable result of their simplistic, impervious makeup. These floating corporate blobs, like the cork's useless presence on the lake, contributed nothing of substance to the healthy ecology of the company. And, akin to the unsinkable drifting cylinder, these men would be the corporate survivors. Meanwhile, beneath the watery surface, the trout would die and the seaweed would eventually decompose, all as part of the life cycle of the lake. Both the fish and the vegetation will have contributed toward making the lake a living, vibrant sea of life—their purpose far nobler than the cork's.

The sun continued its lazy ascent above the eastern horizon. A stirring of the fresh, dewy air and the newly breaking day seemed to bring to focus the life lessons that Theresa's beloved father had taught her. Her spiritual path was often guided by her "Dad Test," thinking how he'd advise her to navigate through a situation. As if lifted by her departed father's spirit, she now understood the lesson this majestic early-morning scene was offering. She wasn't created to be an aimless cork. There was no way she could bob and sway to the mindless dictates of the big-winded Patriarchy. Just like the fickle breeze, her company's regime blew at one moment from the west, shifting in the next moment to blow from the north, soon followed by another directional change—on and on and on. The Corks at her company would continue to take up space, survive, pollute, nod in supposed fellowship with the changing elements, and float on day after day. Theresa, on the other hand, now knew her days at the office were numbered.

◆

Renee shared some stories of how Informers influenced several different workplaces during her career. She vividly recalls her first and subsequent encounters with an Informer.

Informers

One day, while having lunch in the office cafeteria, Renee noticed a message on the lunchroom bulletin board.

Looking for car-pool partner living south of the office
Call Chloe at 555-8733 or extension 835

After tearing off one of the dangling strips listing the two numbers, Renee returned to her desk, dialed 835, and reached Chloe, who worked in the Human Resources Department. As luck would have it, she lived in an apartment building a scant mile away from Renee. Discussing the possibilities of sharing driving responsibilities, they decided to give the car-pool idea a shot. So, with the understanding that one person would drive for the entire week and then the other drive the next week, the car pooling started.

It seemed like a perfect situation. Now both women could cut their gas costs in half. Having a comrade during the often-congested rush hour made the commute more pleasant, and it certainly made the drive seem faster. They took turns bringing favorite CDs of the latest popular music; occasionally, the old classics like Frank Sinatra or early Beatles would blast from the car stereo. Recipes, babies, husbands, favorite movies—all became lively conversation topics during their twice-daily drive. Occasionally, work subjects bubbled to the top.

Chloe, an administrative assistant in her department, reported directly to the vice president of human resources. Apparently, Chloe really liked her job and was excited that she was succeeding in ingratiating herself with Raymond, her boss. One day, she revealed that he asked her to "keep your ear to the ground" and let him know what people were saying and doing.

"But why did he ask you?" Renee quizzed.

"Oh, he figures I get around the office a lot and eat out with people from other departments. Guess I'm in the loop."

"What would he do with the information?"

"I don't know. I suppose he just likes to know what's going on."

"But," Renee continued to probe, "doesn't it make you wonder why he doesn't circulate around the office himself and get information that way?"

"Well, not particularly. Plus, I kinda like being in his confidence. It gives me an edge."

"Yeah, but Chloe, isn't that like spying?"

"Not really. Look, Renee, I told you only because I thought I could trust you!" Chloe snipped.

Perhaps, but now I don't feel as if I can trust you! Renee thought to herself.

Discomforted by Chloe's revelation, Renee decided that carpooling wasn't such a good idea after all. So, after changing her flextime work hours, she informed Chloe that they'd need to drive separately; their schedules no longer meshed.

Chloe, was the first Informer Renee had encountered in the corporate world. Over time, she met others.

As years passed, Renee achieved officer status. To her disappointment, she continued running into people who brownnosed their way into the offices of powerful people and promoted their agendas at the expense of good, hardworking Seeds and Diamonds.

"If I thought Chloe's type was rare, I was proven wrong!" Renee commented. "It seemed that, regardless of where I worked or at what level, there were people who operated with a self-interest that ignored, for want of a better term, fair play. Working with one particular woman, nicknamed 'Kistie', was both personally and professionally challenging."

Kistie, from the Planning Department, was a classic Informer. Kistie's soft-spoken and seemingly gentle style completely masked her manipulative, power-seeking drive. As a new hire, it didn't take her long to prove that she was hopelessly difficult to work with. An employee in Renee's department, Adam, found his projects constantly sabotaged by Kistie, a woman whose entire goal was control and self-promotion. Donald, Adam's counterpart in another department, soon had the same chilling assessment of Kistie: She was nothing but a pain! She continually tangled up assignments by trying to force all projects to pass through her office. What perplexed the two men was how she was never held accountable for the resulting tardy and often mediocre results. They shuddered every time she approached them.

Behind the scenes, Kistie did a great job of playing the misunderstood victim of others' incompetence. A born conniver, she knew that having an executive in her corner was a powerful ace up her sleeve. So, after being counseled by Renee that she was creating unnecessary roadblocks with multiple employees and preventing progress on several assignments, she took her sad story to her boss, Neal, who, in turn, ran to Renee's boss, Jerry, to relay how *Renee* was creating trouble with the staff.

The two men apparently bought Kistie's version of events and fell for her excuses as to why critical projects were behind schedule. In classic Patriarchal style, the two officers encouraged Kistie to let them know if she encountered any other problems. With that invitation, the covert Informer was deputized.

As frictions continued with Kistie, and simple tasks were inexplicably turned into "star wars," Patriarchal wrath surfaced. Citing a pending crisis, Neal called Renee and scheduled a meeting so that he, Renee, and Kistie could talk things over and "clear the air."

At the requested meeting, Kistie projected herself as a bona fide team player, while Neal, who was Renee's peer and fellow officer, listed the problems that Kistie had shared. In Neal's presence, Kistie was a different person—a total phony concealing her meddling, uncooperative nature.

During the exchange, Renee presented her knowledge of the particulars, trying to bring a factual balance to Neal's inaccurate, one-sided perspective. Renee's efforts were in vain. Neal, too weak to question Kistie's propaganda, chose in classic Cork style to remain hoodwinked. He didn't possess the backbone to deal with Kistie by getting the facts, confronting his manipulative employee, and insisting that she get on track and clean up her act. In addition, Renee suspected that Neal and Jerry used this conflict as a way to marginalize her executive status.

Undaunted by the discussion, as the meeting closed, Kistie resurrected her campaign of victimization.

"Before I leave, I'm still confused why you say people find me so hard to work with," she stated, with wide-eyed fake innocence. "No one cares more about results than I do. I just don't understand it." She sighed.

"Kistie, I want you to sit down with Donald and Adam and see if you can work through the upcoming assignments, clarify areas of responsibility and timelines, and then come to a mutual understanding for going forward—have a fresh start," Renee suggested, refusing to excuse Kistie from her liability for the frictions.

After finishing their show-trial effort to patch things up, Neal and Kistie left. As they departed Renee's office, she knew that nothing had been resolved. Clearly, there was a double standard in play, as Kistie was not being held accountable for her actions. Neal proved that he was a useless Cork. Any follow-up to this meeting or further fact-finding was, predictably, not going to occur.

Proving that a leopard doesn't change its spots, Kistie continued to struggle with numerous people. It wasn't until Donald observed her going repeatedly into executive offices and closing the door that her probable role as a spy for the Patriarchy was confirmed—Kistie was an active, full-fledged Informer! Her continuing behavior confirmed the Informer "diagnosis." In group and individual meetings, she began to flaunt her associations, making name-dropping an art. Things worsened when her unwarranted, yet predictable, promotion to director fueled her arrogance. She now operated as both an overt and a covert Informer. The staff couldn't stand her! They knew that every word they uttered would be reworked to suit Kistie's agenda and would be reported straight to the top.

One day, out of the clear blue, Renee was confronted by her boss, Jerry.

"You don't realize how throwing your officer position around affects people. You threaten them with your power, and you think you're better than everyone because of your title!"

"Jerry, where is all this coming from?" Renee asked in disbelief.

"I know what's going on, because it all filters back to me," he snapped.

"But help me understand what this is all about. None of this makes sense! Let's look at the facts."

Jerry didn't care about the facts. Instead, he turned to leave; his parting shot was "Fix it!"

"Looking back," Renee said, "once I realized what Kistie was doing, I should have more aggressively dealt with the situation and proactively presented both Neal and Jerry with factual updates. That might have blunted Kistie's ridiculous and undocumented propaganda. If nothing else, I could have had several conversations with Jerry, when he was less agitated and more open to my input. With good managers, that communication tactic will create positive results. As for Kistie, I should have reeled her in and found some way to utilize her energy in a positive direction.

"In my case, there's more to the story. These events and others confirmed that I was dealing with a boss who had some serious management inadequacies. I'm sure that Jerry used Kistie's sniping as an excuse to attack my leadership. He couldn't fault my job performance, so he milked situations like the Informer episode instead. Kistie played into his hands brilliantly. Over time, it was clear that I was in a pervasively dysfunctional work environment."

◆

If you want to witness the microcosm of corporate personalities, Ginny, a corporate officer, recommends attending an off-site business meeting and watching the upper echelon's dynamics.

Soakers and Smokers

"Our annual planning meeting was set in the plush surroundings of a first-rate country club. It had a large, well-appointed meeting room and, for after-hours gatherings, spa-like amenities. Having finished dinner, we adjourned to begin a casual evening of fellowship. With both a pool and a hot tub available, most of the guys changed into swimsuits, reconvened at the patio, and formed into little cliques. I was there with two other women and approximately twenty men.

"Our president and his closest buddies commandeered the hot tub and sat in the steaming water sipping cognac, lighting cigars, grandly blowing smoke rings, chuckling at jokes—holding an exclusive séance. It was an amazing sight to watch how those not included in the inner circle maneuvered, trying to make their presence known. These outsiders would approach the tub, offer to go for drinks, try to make a joke, and even sit near the tub's edge, but they faced the frustration of not being invited to join the cadre's fun. Obviously, the three women in the group were completely ignored.

"Maureen, an Informer who often claimed that she rubbed shoulders with the Patriarchy, grabbed a cigar, approached the in crowd, and attempted to join them." Ginny recalled, "Her lighting up a big stogie looked ridiculous, and her social efforts proved futile; she was clearly unwelcome. Leslie and I could only roll our eyes at Maureen's awkward attempts to be 'one of the guys.' It had an artificial air and came across as both desperate and totally out of place. I chuckled, as I could sense that the 'Soakers and Smokers' hoped the other female executive and I wouldn't, like Maureen, try to penetrate their clique. They wanted no female intrusion into their circle of fun! Aside from Maureen, they had nothing to fear. Joining their junior high school antics held no appeal for Leslie and me and turned off some of the more grounded, mature men in the group as well. Instead, the two of us, joined by a few male friends, sat at a poolside table, sipped an after-dinner drink, and continued to watch the unfolding activity.

"One of the most amusing events was when Bob, the president, left the steaming tub to visit the changing-house bathroom. In a pathetic gesture, Carl, one of the spurned attendees, ran and staked a spot outside the bathroom door. When Bob re-emerged, Carl 'accidentally' ran into him, verbally gushing in an effort to engage Bob in conversation, all the while pretending to have inadvertently crossed the president's path. We could only marvel at the clumsy effort; it was a pathetic, desperate—almost sad—behavior.

"Carl wasn't alone trying to get Bob's attention. As the evening progressed and more drink was consumed, the scenario became increasingly exaggerated, as self-restraint was less in check. The hot tub setting reminded me of the fabled 'smoke-filled rooms', where fat cats make arbitrary, self-serving business decisions that control people's fate. The pretense and arrogance of Bob and his cronies were disillusioning. I was left with no doubt that psychological manipulation is one of the Patriarchy's most potent tools.

"Throughout the evening, all I could do was be amazed that grown, intelligent men were capable of such pretense and exclusion. I said to myself: 'And to think these are the leaders of our company!'"

◆

The medical field also holds examples of the challenges women face, even though they work with well-educated, highly respected practitioners. A female physician's wealth of experience and insights not only validates the impacts the Patriarchs and Diamonds can have on an organization but also illustrates the influence of disgruntled, mobilized Seeds.

Seed Revolt

As long as Lynn could remember, she wanted to be a doctor, just like her father. With that goal now within reach, she began researching the medical opportunities in several communities located throughout a three-state area. Within a couple months, openings at two regional medical centers and three urban clinics led to multiple interview appointments.

Attracted to a particularly well-known medical establishment, Lynn and her husband accepted the invitation to be guests at the clinic's recruitment dinner. There were two candidates for an opening in the family practice department: Lynn and a male who, like her, recently completed a residency. On paper, the two applicants had virtually identical qualifications. Both came from a family of physicians, both had an impressive grade point average, and both had their MD credentials from the same institution. It was a dead heat.

The format for the dinner was simple: The candidates and their spouses sat at separate round tables, joined by their respective host doctor and wife. Throughout the evening, each of the eight doctors in the family practice was to stop by the candidate's table to get acquainted, visit, and schmooze. An hour into the evening, Lynn and her husband had an uneasy feeling that something was out of sync. Before the recruitment dinner ended, they knew that forces were at play that didn't bode well for her candidacy. While two couples did approach Lynn's table for casual conversation, clearly the remaining six members of the medical staff had no intention of introducing themselves, let alone spending time with the female candidate. Uneasily, Lynn noted that as the evening progressed, the other aspirant had been approached by the entire team of doctors.

The camaraderie, hearty handshakes, and backslapping at the next table made her stomach turn.

"My God, they're provincial!" she said in disbelief, once safely inside the car as it left the parking lot. "I felt totally shunned tonight. I don't care if they do offer me a position, which I know they won't. That's not an environment for me!" Her husband agreed. He, too, felt like a second-class citizen as the evening turned into a nightmare. "How sad," he added. "They clearly favored the other guy without even getting to know you."

Not surprisingly, Lynn was passed over for the position.

Moving on, after several successful interviews and two viable offers, she chose a position at a health center in a large, urban setting. Her practice grew quickly, as she found herself the physician of choice for a surprising number of women, who welcomed the rare opportunity to have a female doctor. Numerous men became regular patients of Lynn's as well. With her schedule filled, it was evident that Lynn's rapport and empathy were highly marketable and made her a standout. In terms of production, she was on top. But beneath the surface, dynamics with the other doctors were less than rosy.

A personal health crisis temporarily necessitated her cutting back on the thirty-six-hour call shifts, per the written instructions of her neurologist. Thus, Lynn approached the scheduler, Dennis, to ask him to make the prescribed adjustments to her on-call hours. With no explanation, he refused to accommodate the request.

Rather, Dennis stated, if Lynn wanted her hours changed, it was up to her to call the other doctors and negotiate the swaps.

"But this doesn't make sense!" she protested, knowing that it was the scheduler's job to make provisions for any situation necessitating a change in assignments.

"Then take your case to the medical director," Dennis retorted.

Gathering her medical documents as proof of her enforced work restrictions, she approached Fred, the medical director, to explain the predicament. Unmoved, his response was the same: "Call the doctors yourself and ask them to trade hours. We can't take time to worry about these kinds of exceptions. It's up to you!"

"To this day, I still get steamed every time I think of the callous way they treated me," Lynn states. "I was dealing with a personal medical situation that seriously threatened my long-term health, but neither Dennis nor Fred gave a damn. While some of the doctors did nothing to help me out, thankfully a couple of the others gladly traded call times with me. I'll always remember the draining exhaustion I felt, while flat on my back in bed, having to track down replacements. One doctor friend was aghast when I reached him; he couldn't believe that it was I, rather than Dennis on the phone, sorting through all the on-call hours."

"Lynn, why in God's name are they having you make these arrangements?" he exclaimed.

"Those words ring in my head to this day. We both knew it was ridiculous," Lynn added.

The insult was compounded when, within the same year, another member of her physicians' team sought an adjustment, as Lynn had earlier, to his call hours. While he personally had no health issues, a member of his family was ill.

"Guess what? Dennis rallied the troops, made all the rescheduling calls, and fully accommodated this guy's request—and unlike me, he didn't have a doctor's orders to cut back his schedule!"

Once her medical crisis passed, Lynn focused on her practice for the next several years, glad to return to a "normal" workweek. Continuing her successful work with patients and maintaining a filled schedule, she was in full stride at the clinic.

A career opportunity surfaced when Fred, the medical director, gave notice of his pending departure to another health care system. Studying the internal posting of the soon-to-be-vacant management position, Lynn knew she was fully qualified for the responsibilities. Deciding to enter the competition, and as part of her methodical approach to submit her application, Lynn contacted the president, Arnold, to indicate her interest in the opening. Asking for the evaluation criteria and other relevant details, she was met with cold, discouraging words.

"Arnold literally stonewalled all my efforts to gather information and apply for the posting. There was no way he was going to help me; he wasn't even subtle about it. He refused to give me the time of day. This was around ten years ago when, at the time, I was still the only female out of thirteen doctors in my department.

It was obvious that only one thing was blocking my aspirations: I was a woman! This incident further reinforced my suspicion that my particular care-giving traits weren't valued. While women patients would seek me out for psychological and medical concerns that require a lot of time commitment to handle, my partners were shying away from that particular care need. To them, this avenue of treatment had little monetary value.

"During those years, I led a solitary existence. As if it wasn't enough to be cut off from the closed male clique, I was also made to feel like an odd duck! I just didn't fit their mold."

Meanwhile, Arnold had growing problems that eclipsed his chauvinist issues with Lynn. Although he enjoyed the endorsement of most of the doctors, he was up to his eyeballs with support-staff issues. The root of the unrest was traceable to his striking a deal with the Seeds. He had offered several of them a bargain. If they would take on a few additional tasks so that he didn't have to hire additional staff until the next fiscal year, he'd give them a year-end bonus to compensate them for their increased time commitment and responsibility.

Rising to the occasion, the selected Seeds pitched in to bail the clinic out of its work backlog. They skimped on lunch hours, came in early, and generally did whatever they could to support the agreement. This additional year-end payment was a welcome holiday spirit-lifter.

The end of December came and went—no bonus checks appeared. Concerned, a few employees met with Arnold to double-check as to when the promised cash would materialize. To their amazement, he indicated that the bonus had not been approved by the Board. Foolishly, Arnold assumed that by blaming the Board for the bad news, he'd be off the hook. But as the truth emerged, it became clear that not only had Arnold overstepped his bounds by making the compensation promise, he had also made no effort to communicate the Board's decision to the Seeds once his strategy was overruled. When all his deceit surfaced, the Board was furious, the Seeds were mad, and Arnold was in trouble.

The impact of his duplicity quickly became evident. Lunch-room grumblings grew into a petition, which, in turn, led to a full-scale revolt of the Seeds. Once they mobilized, the productivity of the clinic staff was in serious jeopardy. Without their committed performance, services at the clinic began to decline noticeably. Responding to the unexpected groundswell of anger, the Board had only one option: Arnold had to go. By mid-February, the besieged president "resigned."

But the Seeds weren't satisfied yet. They wanted the replacement president to have a completely different profile from the irritating, small-minded, conniving, and arrogant Arnold. With that mandate, a desperate Board turned to John, a physician whose leadership and personal qualities were undeniably first-rate.

"The Board wasn't being magnanimous; their collective feet were held to the fire, and they had no choice," Lynn recalls. "They needed to bring in someone totally different from Arnold to overcome all the bad feelings. Apparently, this wasn't the first time he had burned some bridges. It was a unique experience, witnessing the force of the enraged and mobilized staff. Typically, you rarely hear from them. But as they increasingly felt abused and taken for granted, they became a revolutionary power. Their sheer numbers forced the top management to take notice and fix the mess."

Luckily for the clinic, John was a Diamond and the right person to mend fences. With his arrival, a new sheriff was in town. If any doctor or staff member didn't pull his weight, John wasn't shy about disciplining or replacing the individual, if necessary. His drive for excellence was rooted in fairness and openness. When two physicians, rumored to be allies of Arnold, departed, John, a classic gender-blind Diamond, hired the best talent he could recruit: two females. With relief, Lynn found her work environment increasingly reflecting an enlightened management style.

"Coming to work became a real joy. A male-oriented culture was no longer ruling the roost. Dennis, the infamous scheduler, left shortly after the 'revolt.' The departures of Fred, Arnold, and Dennis, combined with the appointment of John, ushered in a new era. Over time, I felt renewed, as my contributions to the organization were recognized and, for the first time since I joined the clinic, praised. Encouraged by John, I applied for the top post of a newly created department and got it. I'm now the medical director for a recently introduced, state-of-the-art specialty that we've added to the clinic."

Summing up the entire scenario, Lynn added, "Socially, some things remain the same. I'm still on my own, as the guys never invite me or the other two female doctors to their outings. But, at least professionally, I found my perfect niche in the health care field. A few years ago, I started a female support group called Venus-Docs. We meet several times a year to network and support each other's professional aspirations, plus to just have a good time golfing, eating, or occasionally going to the theater."

Lynn added a final thought. "For twenty years, I've kept a saying on my refrigerator that, for me, says it all."

When I stand before God at the end of my life, I would hope that I would not have a single bit of talent left and could say, *I used everything you gave me.*

—Erma Bombeck

◆

Office behaviors and the resulting workplace styles are not black and white, rather they come in shades of gray. To put it another way, people's reactions typically fall along a continuum; it's how people conduct themselves the majority of the time that places them in a particular camp. Just as a Patriarch can have "Diamond moments," so, too, can a Diamond err in judgment or behavior and, on occasion, lean more toward the patriarchal side of the workplace continuum. When thinking about building your company network, look for individuals whose deeds usually reflect the Diamond side of the chart (see chart on page 90). Although a true Diamond rarely, if ever, moves to the left of the scale, realize that they, too, can have a bad day. Remember that we are all human and make mistakes. What matters is the *intentionality* of the action. If the transgressor behaved "out of innocence," then move on. Focus on the positives when dealing with those who populate the right side of the behavior range.

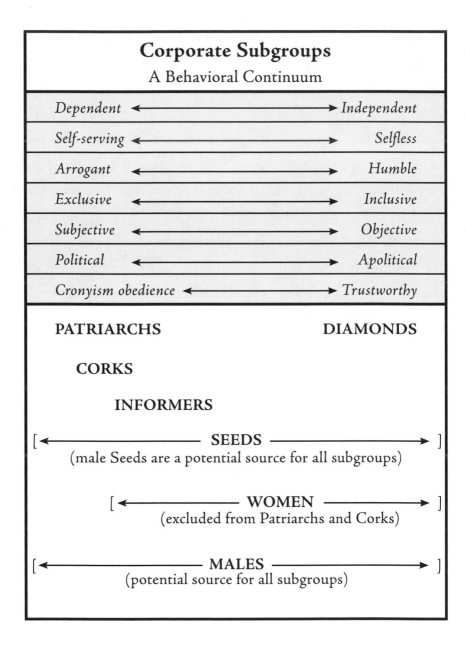

Corporate Subgroups
A Behavioral Continuum

Dependent ←——————————→	Independent
Self-serving ←——————————→	Selfless
Arrogant ←——————————→	Humble
Exclusive ←——————————→	Inclusive
Subjective ←——————————→	Objective
Political ←——————————→	Apolitical
Cronyism obedience ←——————————→	Trustworthy

PATRIARCHS   **DIAMONDS**

CORKS

INFORMERS

[←——————— SEEDS ———————→]
(male Seeds are a potential source for all subgroups)

[←——————— WOMEN ———————→]
(excluded from Patriarchs and Corks)

[←——————— MALES ———————→]
(potential source for all subgroups)

Choices

When we honor the belief that we always have a choice, life shows up differently around us.

—Dottie Gandy and Marsha Clark
Choose! The Role That Choice Plays in Shaping Women's Lives

◆

Life is like a supermarket. Think back to the last time you were in the cereal aisle. Have you ever seen so many options for fulfilling such a basic need as your morning meal? Move on to products for lunch, dinner, entertaining, cleaning, and personal needs—you make choices about these fundamentals every time you cruise past the multitude of product-laden shelves.

There are food products that are healthful and good for your nutritional balance on one end of the continuum, and, at the opposite end, there are items that raise cholesterol, have empty calories, and essentially have no redeeming value other than that they taste good—and provide short-term gratification. The choice is yours. How do you decide, and how much time do you spend reviewing your selection? What are your criteria for choosing? Eat healthy and therefore protect and promote your physical well-being, or be a junk-food junkie with possible long-term consequences. Ideally, there's a bit of balance between your choices; occasionally, your meal selection isn't going to be the wisest, because we all need a "treat" now and then. But some ongoing selections may be downright harmful. When all is said and done, if you strive to make good decisions about your diet the majority of the time, the end result is usually good health. Making a choice is not an exact science.

Take this analogy and apply it to the personal and business decisions you make throughout a lifetime. One thing is certain—you are faced with multiple choices that significantly steer your career path throughout life's journey. What are your criteria for choosing?

How much time do you spend analyzing your options? Did you ever realize, when making your decisions, that there were so many choices that you control?

Return to Ellen's story and her disturbing realization, while sitting in a plush corporate jet, that she had become unrecognizable to herself, a stranger to her own upbringing and values. Ellen continued her story by telling of many thoughtful, analytical decisions she had made during her work and home life over the years. Then she further conveyed the human toll she experienced from her continuous push against the Glass Wall in her workplace culture, which conflicted with her value system. She became physically ill on a regular basis and grappled with chronic mental exhaustion. Her decision not to leave was, in essence, a choice to stay. In hindsight, the problem becomes clear: being surrounded by Glass Walls prevents the needed reflection of your own image.

Ellen went on to describe an event that occurred a few weeks later, after her momentous self-discovery aboard the corporate plane.

Ellen's Choice

Ellen and the major executives of her team gathered with the top client of her firm to discuss a new multiyear agreement. This meeting was essential to retaining the business. Following a full day of presentations and negotiations, the two sides gathered for a formal dinner. Present were the top echelons from both organizations. Ellen was responsible for ensuring that both the meeting and the subsequent dinner were successful.

After a grueling six-hour session that left everyone drained, and with definite creative tensions in the air, the elite members reconvened in the extravagant private dining room of a prestigious hotel. The seating arrangement was carefully calculated to facilitate conversations among the right "top to tops." Most of the individuals had never met one another, a fact camouflaged by the overfriendly and gratuitous conversations.

During the multicourse dinner, Ellen surveyed the long, sumptuous table from end to end and observed the room.

"All I could think, despite all my best efforts to the contrary, was that this is not real!" Ellen recalled. "There was absolutely no authenticity to the evening. There was the proverbial white elephant in the room, but it appeared to go unnoticed. The thought in my head that kept repeating itself over and over again, literally giving me chills, was that I am spending the better part of my life in a game of pretend. The choice I was making to stay, initially one I thought I was making so that I could make a difference, was, in reality, one that was actually changing me—and not for the good."

It was a catharsis. At that precise moment, Ellen realized she could and had to let it all go; she made the difficult decision to leave the company. She knew she had come to a juncture in her life where she had to walk away from a two-decade career with a prestigious company, a generous salary, and associates who had become friends over the years and a big part of her identity. None of these trappings were more important than recovering her soul.

"It was the toughest choice of my career. But the operative word here is *choice*. It was absolutely right for me. Had I decided to stay, I would have made the choice to stick with an unhealthy situation, be a pretender, and face whatever future consequences came my way. That would have made me unrecognizable not only to myself, but also to the people I care about most. Instead, I took my personal power back."

◆

Many of the women we interviewed sprinkle the word *survive* throughout the recounting of their experiences. Sentences would begin, "If I can just get through . . ." You fill in the blanks. Strong, confident women are not quitters. They have countless examples of persevering through the toughest of times. It has been this perseverance that has made them successful and taken them to new heights. Women reach an important turning point, when they realize that there is healthy perseverance and destructive perseverance. If you make the choice to leave a company, does that mean that the Patriarchy's propaganda is accurate that women executives can't take the heat? Does it mean the Patriarchy has "won" and women have "lost"? Absolutely not! It means an informed decision has been made.

It's about choice, and it's always yours to make. Even if you unexpectedly find yourself on the receiving end of job elimination, you still hold the power to select your next steps.

It's your choice to assess the environment you are in and find ways to adapt or influence change, so that others can follow in your steps more successfully. It is absolutely critical to the process to establish your own boundaries. It becomes too easy to get caught up in the day-to-day agendas, thereby failing to protect and honor yourself. Coping with all the complex forces can cause you to lose sight of where you will and will not go. As a consequence, over time, the lines of your value system become blurred, and you begin to feel like you are traveling through a foreign country without a map. Whether it's choosing how to deal with Informers, managing the Patriarchy, or mining for mentors, seek to clarify your path. Know what direction you want to travel in, tell others, and most important, write it down. Taking these actions will allow others to assist and support you and will ensure that you not only own your *own* choices but you *live* them. Become proactive, fully self-actualized—the architect of your future.

Survival Tactics

The way I see it, if you want the rainbow,
you gotta put up with the rain.

—Dolly Parton

◆

The personal accounts in this book are only a few of the chronicles shared by dozens of women representing a large spectrum of professions. These women had impressive credentials, including breaking through the Glass Ceiling. But after reaching the upper echelons of executive management, not one woman found her male peers fully accessible. The Glass Wall theory has been confirmed time and time again by those who lived it.

The good news is that the participants in our study survived, in varying fashion, the Glass Wall experience. Many entered a second stage in their professional careers that brought them continued success and, in most cases, inner peace. Female executives don't mince their words. There was a lot of pain and self-doubt along the way. However, most conclude that the "ride was worth it."

Out of the diverse encounters with workplace challenges faced by women, instructive wisdom eventually surfaces and begins to make some sense out of the chaos. Below is a summary of the Glass Wall survivors' discoveries.

Diamonds

Believe it or not, there are many leaders out there who are true gems. Diamonds are heroes. They make tough decisions for the right reasons and value their people. They are gender-blind. Find one! If you have the good fortune to work for one, learn everything you can from your Diamond. Diamonds can be male or female. They are the best coaches and mentors in the workplace. Corporate

America would have better results if Diamonds took over the reins of power at all levels of business.

Patriarchs

Most business organizations foster a clique of men, Patriarchs, who form a self-serving leadership fraternity. Don't even try to join the Patriarchs, let alone beat them. Your best strategy is to focus on your own professional excellence and objectively determine if it's worth trying to outlast some of them. Focus on keeping them informed, so as to maximize your networking opportunities. In organizations where job performance counts, if they don't deliver a positive performance, these men will, at some point, have to move on to other companies—taking some of their cronies with them. Deal conservatively with these men; never confide any of your corporate observations to the Patriarchy. They can hurt you.

Informers

Informers can be male or female. But female Informers typically use their spying services or bullying techniques to gain an access to the Patriarchy that otherwise, due to their gender, would be denied. It's "heady." They are seeking attention and acceptance from the bigwigs. Because Informers are welcomed into the executive spymaster's office, they falsely believe that they are part of the male in-crowd. This sense of belonging is further reinforced if the Informers are rewarded with promotions or other perks. In the long run, the Informers' fatal flaw is their burning of countless bridges in the workplace. Their resulting isolation is what they deserve, due to their self-serving agenda. Whether dealing with covert or overt Informers, your best tactic is similar to that of coping with the Patriarchy. Focus on your performance and what you can control, or be prepared to move on. Always have a Plan B in mind, as you never know if their espionage is endangering your job security. If you have to deal with these poisonous individuals, remember that you don't have to like them; you just have to work with them. With open eyes, utilize their talents and avoid being perceived as a threat.

Corks

Corks are professionally benign males who specialize in changing with the wind, supporting whatever notion or leader is currently in ascendancy. They are mindless chameleons who bring neither leadership nor value to their positions and, by their passive enabling, allow corporations to take countless wrong turns. The only "success" these individuals can claim is their remarkable record of survival, due to their chronic head bobbing in agreement. Never count on Corks for advice or help, as their opinions are not based on solid insight but rather corporate dogma. Corks are intellectual and emotional lightweights who offer limited value to their companies. As with all individuals, endeavor to add Corks to your list of supporters; their approval can be useful.

Seeds

Seeds offer tremendous resources and can be valuable allies if treated fairly. Be accessible to the group, and harvest their nuggets of wisdom. They are the farm team for future Diamonds or, if inclined to go astray, for Corks, Informers, and the Patriarchy. Try to separate the chaff in this group and find the valuable Seeds.

Safe Harbors

Everyone needs a reliable, empathetic ear—someone to whom you can bare your soul and who, in turn, will be respectful and honest. Ideally, you should find a safe harbor outside of your office, someone who is not your spouse. Although spouses can be marvelous sounding boards, use them sparingly so your home life isn't filled with the tensions from the challenging days at work. Both you and your mate need a break. Even though it's fine to have a close friend at work, be aware that if a workplace associate changes allegiance, what you thought was a safe harbor can turn into a rocky shoal. If you must confide in an office mate, find a trustworthy Diamond. Network with men and women outside your company. Become a safe harbor for someone in need. Never break a confidence (unless someone is in danger). You don't deserve the security of a safe harbor if you aren't one as well.

The Dad Test

The Dad Test is about finding a higher standard to guide decisions and relationships. If you have a person in your life who personifies a reliable moral compass, envision his or her advice when you face tough situations.

Myth of Self

Don't believe in your own myth. In other words, once you focus on your own personal glory, you start to sacrifice job performance and human depth. Greed and arrogance are attractive to no one.

Never Hire a Clone

Female executives will find it easier to survive if they have a strong staff that delivers outstanding results. That means don't hire clones—people who have the same strengths and, conversely, weaknesses as you have. Instead, see every hiring opportunity as a chance to bring depth to your bailiwick. Diverse thought leads to intellectual fertilization.

Ethics

If you compromise your morals and can't look at yourself in the mirror, any success is hollow.

Network

Having friends and industry associates isn't just for the guys. Line up a group of emotionally healthy female friends, and create your own consortium of advisors. Add males to your network, too, especially Diamonds. This network group can become a vital lifeline and a safe harbor. Check into some of the emerging women's network organizations in your local community.

Balance

Balance, balance, balance. Never forget that your home, personal life, and faith are your anchors.

Perseverance

Think of perseverance as a quality that helps you survive the inevitable tough times so that you can enjoy the positive ones that follow. Understand, however, that perseverance for the sake of perseverance can root you in a disastrous situation from which you should exit. Learn how to differentiate between good perseverance and perseverance that will damage your mental and physical health.

Exit Strategy

Although corporate leaders may eventually self-destruct if they don't deliver results, you need to determine if you can or want to outlast them. The longevity of your nemesis can be partially predicted by examining the Board of Directors. If that body is inundated with either Corks or Patriarchal pals, it will be hard to outlast the leadership in the inner sanctum. Have a professional Plan B, and be open to acknowledging that sometimes the battle is just not worth the cost. Move on. As a publishing friend says: "If you can't join them, leave them!" Sometimes, it just makes good sense for your mental health. If possible, be aware of severance package options, as they can influence your strategy and timing for leaving the organization.

If you lose your job:

- **Allow yourself time to grieve.**

- **Recalibrate your soul.** Reflect on the accomplishments that gave you genuine fulfillment. You may discover that, in the final analysis, closing the big deals or other business achievements take on a new, more balanced and less important perspective. Inner peace is life's ultimate reward.

- **Forgive yourself.** We all make *a lot* of errors in how we react to people and situations. Don't beat yourself up for not having the perfect response or action every time you were confronted with challenges. Find comfort in knowing that you tried to do your best with the cards you were dealt.

- **Learn from your mistakes.** All your experiences, both good and painful, increase your depth of character and add to your personal and professional skills. To quote Rosalind Russell: "Flops are a part of life's menu, and I've never been a girl to miss out on any of the courses." In a more serious vein, Eleanor Roosevelt reminds us: "The only man who makes no mistakes is the man who never does anything." Mistakes are an essential component to being an achiever and, most of all, being human.

- **Remember that the sun will come up tomorrow.** Like the sun, you must also rise up and move on.

- **Take charge of your future.** You *will* survive *if* you make the choice to do so.

And finally:

Heart

At the end of the day, be proud of who you are. If you choose to work outside of the home, care enough about the human side of your job to mentor and uplift others in your workplace. Strive to be a Diamond, and shepherd other people through their tough times. What goes around comes around!

The Mosaic Masterpiece

So often I have listened to everyone else's truth
and tried to make it mine. Now, I am listening deep
inside for my own voice, and I am softly, yet firmly,
speaking my own truth.

—Liane Cordes
The Reflecting Pond: Meditations for Self-Discovery

◆

A re we glad to have spent so many years in corporate America, and, if given the chance, would we do it all over again? Absolutely. Thanks to the classic school of hard knocks, we've benefited immeasurably from all the experiences and people we met along the way. These priceless learning opportunities have made us more realistic, insightful, and durable. We know that, regardless of the industry, situations with the Patriarchy and Informers will continue to challenge us; but the next time around, we'll be more secure in how to work with the ego-driven and insecure people who cruise through the corridors of every company.

Our combined fifty-plus years of experience have been a priceless education. Doing it over again, we would make the same *moral* choices—but we'd strive to deliver our message more effectively and do a better job to, as President Ronald Reagan once said, "disagree without being disagreeable." If a former president of the United States could recognize the value of different perspectives, why can't CEOs and other ivory-tower leaders understand that divergent thought delivered by diverse people is enriching and has great organizational value? Great leadership welcomes wisdom from a variety of sources, synthesizes the data, and finds a higher, better paradigm. President Reagan lived by the standard, so quickly forgotten by today's political leadership as well as corporate executives, that you can have a different opinion but remain a friend, a resource. Diamonds get it; the Patriarchy doesn't.

There are many Beccas, Ellens, and Dianes out there. Every day, women are facing the Glass Ceiling. Be assured, breaking past the Ceiling *does* occur. But the secret to survival is to not throw in your professional towel when facing the surprise discovery that, after breaking through one glass barrier, you now bump against another—the Glass Wall.

Upon reflection, a truth emerges: the experiences in our careers shape our lives as women. This axiom applies to our existence in the business setting as well as in our daily lives. The good, bad, and ugly all contribute to uncovering our potential and true selves. Because we spend so much of our time on earth in pursuit of our careers, our professional environment often becomes a dominant determinant of who we are and, potentially, who we become. Character development and personal growth often come with a price.

Each of us has become a "Mosaic Masterpiece." All our "weathering" before, during, and after entering the inner sanctum hasn't destroyed us at all. Instead, our character has been developed and honed to an entirely new level of self-actualization. The countless bits and pieces of our business experience, combined with the enriching tapestry and texture of our lives at home, along with treasured friends and countless industry associates have created two more well-rounded, eclectic, and—yes—happy women.

As you navigate the corporate labyrinth, keep your high standards; continue to care about your company's people and its success. Above all else, win the ultimate battle by making decisions that are right for you—the choices that make you feel good every morning when you wake up and look in the proverbial mirror. Through appropriate perseverance, we hope you will realize, as we did, that every little shard of struggle, every small piece of shattered hope can be combined, piece by piece, into a new and beautiful work of art.

Going forward, find your Diamonds, both male and female, and, like them, become a safe harbor for those still enduring the passage. Gather all the precious fragments of your experience and emerge as a Mosaic Masterpiece. Then, most important of all, continue the journey.

Epilogue
Glass Wall Sisterhood

Organizations focused on women's issues are emerging throughout the country. These consortiums come in a variety of forms: some are exclusively for female membership; others admit both sexes. During the last decade, there has been a proliferation of groups that offer women valuable networking, professional seminars, and a social connection. Some of these groups are nationwide organizations and can be easily contacted via the Internet. Other informal and local associations are gaining momentum within many communities. University and college organizations specifically geared to alumnae are another valuable resource. These educational entities offer a relatively easy comfort threshold, thanks to the graduate members sharing a common school culture and experience.

For individuals less inclined to join an organization, gathering friends and creating a group that is primarily social but open to discussing, even researching, business concerns can be an emotional lifesaver. Ideally, by creating a regular schedule for getting together, this valuable set of allies can gain momentum and become an on-call advisory group.

Isolated female executives attest that one of the worst office situations they endure is their sense of feeling utterly alone, even shunned, in the workplace. This emotional challenge can be better managed if you realize that it's often necessary to look *outside* your company for colleagues to fill your professional and social voids. Although you can't "fix" the workplace modus operandi of the Patriarchy, you can reduce its grinding effect by finding camaraderie and support in other places. Networking is a healthy, proactive choice that can provide emotional sustenance for women coping with Glass Walls.

Regardless of which networking route you choose to take, the opportunity to draw from the expertise of others and be part of a group that provides a support structure is a valuable survival tool.

◆

Imagine a scene in which five women who are meeting for a monthly social dinner share their workplace experiences. Although the following scenario and some of the stories are fictionalized, much is based on situations that actually occurred.

The Glass Wall Discovery

The monthly "Meet and Eat Night" was held, as usual, on the third Thursday at the Café Cirque. The now-regular group would be there—Angela, Barb, Mandy, Debra, and Jane. The women now counted on this dinner ritual as the one predictable time each month that they could get together to enjoy female companionship, share career highs and lows, compare notes on child rearing, laugh at countless stories, empathize, and offer advice.

Debra, first to grab the corner table, sat dejectedly, waiting for the other four to join her. With unabated frustration, she felt that she finally had met a day that was more than she could bear. As Angela, Mandy, and Jane joined her, they could see that Debra's mood was anything but her usual sparkling self. If anyone could spin a tale and make the troops laugh, it was Debra. But tonight, the usual Debra was nowhere to be seen. Instead, the Debra they saw was slouched at the table and clearly troubled.

"When Barb gets here, I've got to tell you about a day that beats all! Believe me, fact is stranger than fiction."

"Well, thankfully, I'm not alone when it comes to feeling frustrated. On a scale of 1 to 10, today ranked a 1 for being the most irritating day I've had in years. The only reason it didn't score a zero is because I'm still breathing!" moaned Mandy. "It's a good thing I can decompress here before going home—with this mood, I'd walk straight through the door without opening it first!"

Angela complained, "Look, try using your intelligence in a room full of men jockeying for favor with the CEO, while telling absurd, off-color jokes. Their idea of good decision-making procedures and mine aren't even in the same galaxy!"

As Barb approached her friends sitting at their usual table, their collective stress telepathically smacked her. *Good grief, what's this all about? Speeding ticket? IRS audit?* "What's this ugly mood I'm sensing? You guys look terrible. This doesn't appear to be my definition of a lighthearted Meet and Eat Night at all! I was hoping this group would make up for my less-than-stellar day at work. We'd better order before they throw us out for ruining the ambiance."

After quickly ordering, the women turned to Debra, who was first in line with her bad-day experience.

"I've got first dibs on *the* losing event of the day, so get comfortable and prepare to be amazed!" Obviously troubled, Debra launched into how she had been called into a meeting with the owner of her brokerage. Out of nowhere, he announced that she was stepping on his feet. She had topped his sales numbers, and their managerial differences further aggravated the situation. "Get a load of this. He proceeded to tell me that there can be only one chief, and he has decided it's going to be him! Even though I was hired to create and manage a sales team, plus have clients of my own, he feels I'm now becoming too big for my britches, since clients are requesting that I take on their accounts. My God, I thought, he's getting the best sales and margins he's ever had; I've actually taken his company from red to black. But what was driving the whole conversation is that he's jealous, and his entrepreneurial ego won't accept other ideas and perspectives!! To cap it off, he told me he's going to start spending more time on the sales side, *and* he's giving me two weeks' notice!!"

A collective gasp pierced the air.

"Not once did he ever level with me and tell me my job was on the line. Not once did he thank me for the profit his company was beginning to rake in. He used me to clean up the mess, set the course straight, and train the new sales staff—and now I'm expendable!!!"

"You mean no one in that organization ever entered your office and expressed any indication that you might be eliminated?" Barb asked in amazement.

"Not once!"

"Well, then, how can he fire you without warning, when you've been such a strong performer?" Jane questioned.

"Simple—he eliminated the position. Surgical assassination. No way to be legally contested. Maybe smart, but in fact, it's ethically reprehensible—a way to save labor costs."

"Oh, my God, your term *surgical assassination* is perfect!" Mandy declared, "I'm seeing this 'elimination of the position' strategy used more and more. Clients contact me all the time to see if they have a valid lawsuit when they're victims. It can be perfectly legal, but if it's not part of a legitimate organizational need to restructure, it's a disgusting abuse of power. Position elimination has become a way to get rid of an employee who doesn't suck up and kowtow to the leadership. I'm finding that perfectly good people can be dismissed, even though they have a superb performance record."

"Oh, Debra, your day *does* beat mine," Angela sympathized. "You know, some men forget we're first-class citizens. If nothing else, had you been a man, your boss probably would have felt less threatened. I mean, come on! If two guys have some sort of issue to settle, I've seen where one guy will suggest to the other guy, "Hey, let's go have a drink and talk about it," or at the very least, they'll have a casual conversation at the office to get the point across. Why can't they do the same for a female employee?"

"It's not a Glass Ceiling—it's a *Glass Wall!*" Suddenly, Barb distilled what, over time, had been happening to each of them. "Think about it. We've broken through the Glass Ceiling and become officers or, in Mandy's case, an attorney. But now that we've earned these high-powered positions, our male peer group still denies us access to their clique and many of the processes of communication and strategizing they enjoy! Every day, in some small way, we're being denied the proverbial level playing field. The Glass Wall describes it perfectly!

"A few months back," Barb continued, "I tried to find Steve, so he and I could touch base about a project. And guess what? Steve and the rest of the vice presidents were off-site in a meeting! It wasn't just some sort of unimportant weekly update—it was for determining the Five-Year Plan!! I was furious. I'm the only female on the executive team, and not only wasn't I invited, it was kept secret from me!

"Then, get this," she added. "A few weeks later, as I sat in a conference room conducting a strategy review, I kept seeing the guys walking out and getting into their cars and taking off for the day. Come to find out, they were off to Atlantic City for another 'meeting.' Give me a break! Once again, the Glass Walls not only excluded me, but the whole trip was hidden from me. I still can't believe how much company money and time their junket probably wasted. But, regardless of my feelings about their Atlantic City spree, what hurts the most is that they spent time together, supposedly making company decisions and intentionally bypassing my input."

"Speaking of Glass Walls," Mandy interjected, as though a lightbulb suddenly turned on in her head, "you all remember how I decided to escape an undesirable environment several years ago. I lined up alternative work options, because I knew my male counterparts weren't giving me a fair shake. I was tired of wasting my energy on the politics and had grown totally frustrated as it became clear that I'd never have a shot at 'Partner.' So, hoping to find a better work environment," Mandy continued, "I joined a new law office. Sadly, the cure was worse than the disease. The male attorneys would offer each other their extra, sometimes high-profile referrals. But they never handed me a plum opportunity. Instead, they'd dump the uninteresting grunt work onto my desk. What a boring way to chalk up billable hours. It may sound like a little thing, but believe me, it got old! To this day, I'm still shocked by how such well-educated men could be so dismissive toward me."

"Mandy," Angela replied, "the smartest move you ever made was starting your own firm!" Mandy nodded in agreement.

Jane had been silent, absorbing the stories while, at the same time, mentally recalling her own Glass Wall situations. "You know," she said after a sip of her pinot noir, "I'm the only corporate vice president who has been denied an on-site support staff. Coincidentally, I'm also the only *female* corporate vice president.

There's clearly a double standard going on here. If one were to do a spreadsheet showing sales volume, profitability, and years of service, I would be number one! I've put in countless requests for additional support and staff, but the other executives have this attitude working against me of 'where can she go and make the same money?' and rationalize 'she's made it without those things so far; why does she need them now?' I get really angry when I have to work faster, harder, and longer than any of my male peers, who are the ones getting the corporate resources! You know, I'm getting tired of dragging my work home every night and every weekend, while the guys, thanks to the efforts of their support staff, can be off attending golf tournaments!"

"And you should be!" agreed Angela. "Let's focus on the bright side. The good news is that we've beaten the odds by successfully advancing our careers. But the bad news is that we're isolated and prevented from fully contributing our talents. Ironically, the females in my company look up to me and think, 'Wow, she's made it!' But they don't see my loneliness or realize that I've broken through one glass barrier only to bump up against another. Face it, there's a very strong male network operating here—and it prevents us from having equal access to what we've rightly earned."

"I think we need to rename ourselves the 'Glass Wall Sisterhood,'" Barb said, half joking, but then a serious look crossed her face. "Think about it, all of us have had firsthand experience with what I call the Glass Wall. That's both astounding and tragic. You know, all this frustration reinforces the importance of our social times together. Who else do we really have to talk with? There's no one at our workplaces. Time and time again, when I've tried to talk with some of the guys in my office, I've been misrepresented and betrayed. Boy, through the school of hard knocks, I've learned that I can't safely share my thoughts about the business with most of them. There's an occasional Diamond in the group who's gender blind and a friend, but that is so rare. When all is said and done, women lack a support structure at work. We need to network just like the men do!"

"Exactly!" Debra agreed. "Look, our sisterhood is a valuable forum and can fill a lot of our needs. Just tonight, I was thinking: thank God for this group! You know, together, we have a lot of collective and valuable experience. Right now, I don't know where I'd be without your support. I've never felt worse yet, at the same time, more embraced."

"Let's take this a step further and be sure we don't hesitate to call one another when we need to talk about anything," Barb suggested. "We need to be available to each other and not just depend on our scheduled dinners for moral support."

"I couldn't agree more!" Debra said with a brightened tone.

The Meet and Eat Night friends, now renamed "The Glass Wall Sisterhood," finished the evening by brainstorming along with Debra as to how she might deal with her termination. They all assured her that a person with her brains and skills can bring a lot of talent to many organizations. They offered priceless, honest validation. Gradually, the mood lifted, as, once again, it was clear that the women not only had a special friendship but also a powerful forum for future networking along business lines.

◆

www.GlassWalls.org

Recognizing the value and need for female networking opportunities, we have created a Web site that offers resources, services, and articles dedicated to supporting women.

Biography

Jean Rostollan is the cofounder of Glass Wall Enterprises, the owner of a consulting business, and an author. During her professional career, Ms. Rostollan spent more than a decade as a corporate executive for a national food service company. She continues actively donating time for church and community service and has served on numerous committees, including the board of directors for a local nonprofit organization. Ms. Rostollan is married, has one daughter, and lives in Burnsville, Minnesota.

Rhonda Levene is the cofounder of Glass Wall Enterprises and currently an executive of a Fortune 100 company. Ms. Levene has spent over twenty years in corporate America, holding executive positions in public and private companies. She lends support to other women through her participation in a national mentoring program and her board involvement with a local nonprofit organization. Ms. Levene is married, has twin sons, and lives in Plano, Texas.